SUCCEEDING
LIKE SUCCESS

The Affluent Consumers of Asia

SUCCEEDING LIKE SUCCESS

The Affluent Consumers of Asia

Yuwa Hedrick-Wong

John Wiley & Sons (Asia) Pte., Ltd.

Other Wiley Editorial Offices

John Wiley & Sons, 111 River Street, Hoboken, NJ 07030, USA
John Wiley & Sons, The Atrium Southern Gate, Chichester P019 8SQ, England
John Wiley & Sons (Canada) Ltd, 5353 Dundas Street West, Suite 400, Toronto, Ontario M9B 6HB, Canada
John Wiley & Sons Australia Ltd, 42 McDougall Street, Milton, Queensland 4064, Australia
Wiley-VCH, Bosch Strasse 12, D-69469 Weinheim, Germany

Library of Congress Cataloging-in-Publication Data

ISBN-13   978-0-470-82210-4
ISBN-10   0-470-82210-4

Wiley Bicentennial Logo : Richard J. Pacifico
Typeset in 12/15 points, Garamond by JC Ruxpin Pte Ltd
Printed in Singapore by Markono Print Media Pte Ltd
10 9 8 7 6 5 4 3 2 1

CONTENTS

FOREWORD

Much has been written about Asia's coming of age across multiple dimensions and the rapid morphing of consumer profiles across the region is an emphatic corroboration of this coming of age. The emergence of women as an empowered and powerful consumer segment, and the rapid expansion of the well-endowed and increasingly youthful elderly consumers are two of the dynamic trends that have been highlighted through our previous research and analyses.

Nothing succeeds like success—this maxim, in spite of being frequently quoted, is truer than ever in the context of Asia's new and dynamic consumer market trends. Burgeoning economic wealth is boosting the ranks of Asia's affluent consumers, redefining not only purchasing patterns and preferences but, more importantly, who is making the purchases.

In this, the third book in the MasterCard Insights series of books drawing on our industry-leading research, Dr. Yuwa Hedrick-Wong, economic advisor to MasterCard in Asia/Pacific, discusses these wealthy consumers across Asia, segmented into affluent (Australia, Hong Kong, Japan, Korea, Singapore and Taiwan) and emerging (China, India, Indonesia, Malaysia, Philippines and Thailand) markets. Across the board, these consumers (sub-divided into the mass affluent and rich households) in all these markets are showing rapid growth. Not only are people wealthier but, more critically, their numbers are growing rapidly. For example, there are estimated to be more than 11 million mass affluent households in affluent Asia and more than 58 million in emerging Asia by 2016, representing an enormous business opportunity of more than $600 billion.

What is of particular significance is the growth of the mass affluent segment in all the key12 markets in Asia/Pacific by the year 2016. Not surprisingly, in China, this will be a pool of more than 44.9 million households. In India, the number will stand at 10.5 million and, in Japan there will be more than 7.1 million households in this segment.

The future size of the affluent consumer market of Asia, as forecasted by Dr. Hedrick-Wong, is impressive and likely to surprise even veteran watchers of this market segment. Dr. Hedrick-Wong has also performed a valuable service in constructing systematically, a set of definitions to categorize the mass affluent and the rich households across Asia/Pacific. In addition, his formulation of the three key pathways to affluence, grounded solidly in the socioeconomic histories of the region of the past 50 years, provides new perspectives to examine and understand who these affluent consumers are and how they may behave as consumers. For the first time, this comprehensive and extensive research sheds light on the evolution of the affluent consumer segment in Asia and provides businesses with vital information on which to base their plans and competitive strategies.

As this book shows, the opportunities to reach out to these consumers are potentially abundant. For businesses, the message is clear—their future success will depend on their ability to forge durable partnerships with these affluent customers.

André Sekulic
President
Asia/Pacific, Middle East & Africa, MasterCard Worldwide

ACKNOWLEDGMENT

Many people have provided thoughtful feedback and constructive criticisms on *Holding Up Half the Sky: The New Women Consumers of Asia* and *The Glittering Silver Market: Rise of the Elderly Consumers of Asia*, the companion volumes to this book. They shared with me their knowledge and insights, and made numerous suggestions for improvement. Many lessons learned have been distilled from these exchanges and some have found their way into this volume. For this I am grateful to Paul Shaw, Maurice Levi, Tan Kong Yam, Manu Bhaskaran, Francis Lui, Jim Walker, Simon Ogus, Martin Soong and Fan Gang. I would also like to thank Barkha Pande and her team of communications professionals at Weber Shandwick for their patient guidance. Last, but not least, the continuing support from André Sekulic and Georgette Tan at MasterCard Worldwide is deeply appreciated.

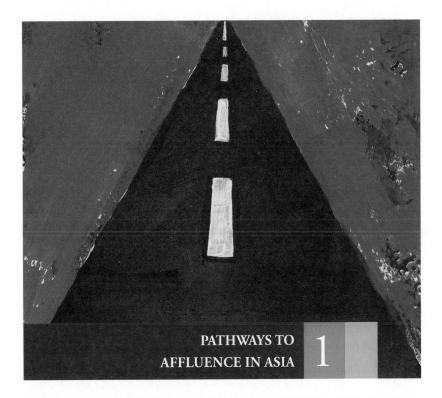

PATHWAYS TO AFFLUENCE IN ASIA 1

Asia's rapid growth since the end of World War II is well known. Most of Asia was dirt-poor at the end of the war, from industrial Japan in the north to the agricultural societies in Southeast Asia. China turned communist and cut itself off from the outside world. Newly independent India adopted a different set of shackles to mire itself in poverty: nationalization of the economy, intrusive regulations and choking bureaucratic red tape. The prospects of rapid economic growth in Asia were decidedly dim in the immediate post-World War II years.

And yet the extraordinary success of East Asia, followed later by Southeast Asia, then China and India in the ensuing five decades, came as a surprise to many, including the specialists and experts who made it their business to know.

One group of authoritative "experts," known as development economists (economists who specialize in the study of how poor countries could become more developed), for example, generally saw Asia as a lost cause in the 1950s and even in the 1960s. As was pointed out by the late economist Lord Peter Bauer at the London School of Economics, many leading development economists at the time believed Asia's growth potential was limited as a result of overpopulation, poor resource endowment, and the negative impacts of war and political instability. Some of these experts even went as far as to suggest that Sub-Sahara Africa stood a much better chance of rapid development and growth.[1] How wrong they were.

The experience of Hong Kong, a British colony until 1997, is particularly instructive. Completely lacking in natural resources, and with its population swelled by a massive influx of refugees escaping political turmoil in mainland China, Hong Kong in the early 1950s resembled more a gigantic refugee camp than the modern metropolis that it is today. The conventional wisdom at the time, as captured by "General Principle Fourteen" of the United Nations Conference on Trade and Development in 1964, was that colonial status is incompatible with economic development and material progress. And yet, Hong Kong, which was a colony for 52 years after the end of World War II, and where seven million people piled into a small space that is not even self-sufficient in water and food—there the per capita income rose from below the sub-Sahara Africa average in the 1950s to make the former colony one of the wealthiest markets in the world today. Hong Kong also has the second-longest life expectancy in Asia after Japan.

Something clearly is wrong with the "experts" and their conventional wisdom. With hindsight, it is evident that there has been an important common thread in the development of Asian countries in the last half a century, regardless of their different conditions: a pragmatic "market friendly" approach to managing their economies. This approach in turn prepared a fertile ground for Asia's entrepreneurs to flourish. Local entrepreneurs adapted to new postwar environments, leveraging every connection to seek out new markets and opportunities. Against the odds many succeeded; some spectacularly. Their efforts also proved beneficial to the society at large. Apart from generating income and employment, many entrepreneurs fostered conditions for others to succeed. In other words, entrepreneurs in Asia have done good by doing well, enriching themselves at the same time that they enriched the Asian region as a whole.

In the coming decade, entrepreneurial energy in Asia will gather even greater momentum. Market liberalization in China and India is unleashing new sources of growth and business opportunities. A rejuvenated Japan with its new and younger generation of business leaders will change how Japan competes. Regional economic integration will shift into high gear, making Asia an even more attractive market for investment and production. The number of Asia's affluent consumers will reach a new critical mass, making the region a glittering jewel in the crown of the world's consumer markets.

To understand the affluent consumers of Asia one must look at their pathways to success, which played an important role in molding their consumption patterns. These pathways are the result of interactions between entrepreneurial drive and the prevailing social, cultural and economic conditions in different parts of Asia. The entrepreneurial pioneers had the most difficult tasks, as they cut through uncharted territory; but their labor benefited not only themselves, but also those who were to follow later. These followers in turn broaden the trail, making it easier still for others to follow. Gradually a well-defined pathway to affluence is formed. Such pathways, however, are always a compromise between the pioneering efforts of the entrepreneurs and the conditions of a given time and place. They embody the struggle between individual ambitions and the social reality of obstacles to success. They leave indelible imprints on those who come through them. Thus, these pathways to affluence are the keys to understanding the values, aspirations, and priorities of the affluent themselves.

FROM RAGS TO PROSPERITY

Asia has been the world's fastest growing region since the end of World War II. Table 1.1 summarizes the average annual growth rates of nominal gross domestic product (GDP) over the 1985 to 2005 period for the 12 key markets in Asia. While the range of growth rates is quite wide, overall growth has been uniformly high. At the low end of the spectrum are the Philippines at 6.4% per year and India at 6.7%. At the high end are Korea and China at 12.2% and 11% respectively. In the post-1997 crisis period, growth has generally resumed or even accelerated in many of the region's markets. In markets where growth has declined post-1997, such as in Hong Kong and Japan, deflation was largely to blame. In any event, growth in both Hong Kong and Japan has resumed significantly since 2004. Japan's recovery from the decade-long stagnation of the 1990s is particularly encouraging, as the country is the second largest economy in the world and the largest in Asia. India's surge from the average of 6.7% annual growth in the last 20 years to 9.5% in the more recent past is especially impressive. The bottom line is that the 12 key markets in Asia had a collective GDP of about $2.5 trillion in 1985. Twenty years later, in 2005, GDP had grown to over $10.4 trillion, averaging an annual growth rate of 7.5%.

Such an extended record of growth has allowed Asia to retain its title as the world's fastest growing region despite the financial crisis of 1997.

Table 1.1

Average Annual GDP Growth Rates (US$ Current prices)

	1985-2005	**1999-2005**
Australia	7.8%	10.1%
China	11.0%	11.9%
Hong Kong SAR	8.8%	1.0%
India	6.7%	9.5%
Indonesia	7.3%	15.6%
Japan	7.0%	2.8%
Korea	12.2%	13.0%
Malaysia	8.0%	9.0%
Philippines	6.4%	5.9%
Singapore	10.4%	5.5%
Taiwan	9.2%	3.3%
Thailand	8.4%	6.3%

(World Bank, World Development Indicators April 2006; for Taiwan: Directorate General of Budget, Accounting and Statistics.)

These growth rates can be translated into per capita terms to take account of the growing populations of these markets. Table 1.2 summarizes the per capita GDP growth rates in three different time periods for comparative purposes: (i) a 20-year period of 1985 to 2005, which is then broken down to (ii) a 15-year period of 1985-1999, representing the period that encompasses the 1997 crisis and its immediate aftermath, and (iii) the five-year period of 2000-2005, representing post-crisis growth.

Korea has the highest average annual growth in per capita GDP over the 20-year period, followed by China, then Taiwan. The Philippines has the lowest annual per capita growth during this period, which is in part a result of its persistently high population growth. In the post-crisis period, however, China's average per capita growth rate at over 12% is highest, followed by Korea's 9.7%. India's growth rate jumped from the pre-crisis 3.2% to an impressive post-crisis 8.1%. Per capita GDP growth has slowed in Taiwan, Thailand, Singapore, Japan and the Philippines in the post-crisis period.

Table 1.2
Per Capita GDP Annual Growth Rates (US$ Current prices)

	1985-2005	1985-1999	2000-2005
Australia	6.5%	5.3%	9.2%
China	9.8%	8.9%	12.1%
Hong Kong SAR	7.5%	10.4%	0.6%
India	4.7%	3.2%	8.1%
Indonesia	5.8%	4.2%	9.4%
Japan	6.7%	9.2%	0.9%
Korea	11.2%	11.9%	9.7%
Malaysia	5.3%	4.8%	6.5%
Philippines	4.1%	4.9%	2.4%
Singapore	7.8%	9.2%	4.5%
Taiwan	8.2%	10.9%	2.0%
Thailand	7.1%	8.1%	4.7%

(World Bank, World Development Indicators April 2006; for Taiwan: Directorate General of Budget, Accounting and Statistics.)

To get a tangible sense of how life has changed for the people in these markets, one has to examine their actual per capita income calculated in US dollar terms, as is done in Table 1.3. In 1985, for example, per capita income in China was a miserably low $288 (in other words, less than $1 per day). This was just a few years after the launch of its "open door" policy. Twenty years later it has risen almost six times to over $1,700.

Per capita income increased by a factor of four in Singapore, rising from $6,500 in 1985 to almost $27,000 in 2005, putting Singaporeans firmly among the wealthiest citizens in the world. The pace of per capita income increase has been similar in Hong Kong. In spite of its relatively high population growth, the per capita income of India rose from $300 in 1985 to over $700 in 2005, and most of the increase happened after the beginning of its economic reform in the early 1990s. For high-income countries such as Japan and Australia, the increase in per capita income has been no less impressive, having grown three times as much in these 20 years.

Table 1.3

GDP Per Capita (US$ Current Prices)

	1985	2005
Australia	10,882	34,714
China	288	1,703
Hong Kong SAR	6,368	25,444
India	300	714
Indonesia	618	1,259
Japan	11,311	35,787
Korea	2,369	16,422
Malaysia	2,026	5,040
Philippines	562	1,159
Singapore	6,485	26,835
Taiwan	3,235	14,476
Thailand	751	2,577

(World Bank, World Development Indicators April 2006; for Taiwan: Directorate General of Budget, Accounting and Statistics.)

The per capita income measure, however, is a statistical artifact that just divides GDP by the number of people. In reality, how income is distributed is as important because massive growth may benefit a minority of a population, leaving the majority as poor as before.

One simple way to assess income distribution is to compare the percentage of income held by the poorest 20% of the population with that held by the richest 20% of the population, as is shown in Table 1.4. The difference between the richest and poorest 20% of the population is shown in the [(b) - (a)] column on the right. A low value in that column, which means that the difference in income between the richest and poorest 20% is small, indicates a more equitable income distribution. As a benchmark measure, data from the US and the UK are included.

According to this measure, Malaysia and the Philippines have the worst income distribution among all the markets compared. The difference between the richest and poorest 20% in Malaysia is 49.9 and in the Philippines 46.9. In contrast, Japan and Korea have the best income distribution, the difference between the richest and poorest 20% of the population being 25.1 and 29.6 respectively. Australia, India and Taiwan are halfway between these two ends of the spectrum, measuring 35.4, 34.4 and 35.3 respectively.

Overall, however, income distribution is quite good in Asia. Only six regional markets have income distribution patterns worse than that of the US, which is measured at 40.4. Three of these six, Thailand, Singapore and China, are only marginally worse than the US. While income distribution is considered fairly equitable in the UK, which is measured at 37.9, it is less equitable than six of the region's markets, however. The generally fairly equitable patterns of income distribution in Asia mean that not only is the size of the middle class relatively large, but that this is also true for the upper middle class, where affluent consumers are found.

Table 1.4

Income Shares Held by the Poorest and Richest 20%

	(a) % of income held by the poorest 20% of population	(b) % of income held by the richest 20% of population	(b) - (a)
Japan	10.6	35.7	25.1
Korea	7.9	37.5	29.6
India	8.9	43.3	34.4
Indonesia	8.4	43.3	34.9
Taiwan	5.7	41.0	35.3
Australia	5.9	41.3	35.4
Thailand	6.3	49.0	42.7
Singapore	5.0	48.9	43.9
China	4.7	49.0	44.3
Hong Kong SAR	5.3	50.8	45.5
Philippines	5.4	52.3	46.9
Malaysia	4.4	54.3	49.9
US	5.4	45.8	40.4
UK	6.1	44.0	37.9

(World Bank, World Development Indicators April 2006; for Taiwan: Directorate General of Budget, Accounting and Statistics.)

As mentioned earlier, this extraordinary record of successful economic growth in Asia is due, in no small measure, to the generally pragmatic and market-friendly policies introduced in the region. In market after market in Asia, such policies were introduced, faster and more effectively in some places and less so in others, but all with astonishingly positive results. This is what the "experts" missed, since many of them harbored anti-market sentiments and were suspicious of the private sector at best, if not outright antagonistic toward it. In South Korea and Taiwan, such market-oriented policies were introduced by governments that could only be described as military dictatorships. China's market opening and reform, launched at the end of the 1980s, had perhaps the most dramatic impact; and it has certainly served subsequently as a positive demonstration of what market liberalization can accomplish, nudging India onto its own path of market reform. In unified Vietnam, where the communist party holds political monopoly, market reform and liberalization are also underway. For the Vietnamese, former enemy number one, the US, is now the number one investor to attract.

These pro-market economic policies proved to have had a profound impact on how entrepreneurial efforts are directed in Asia, and why they have produced such astounding results. As pointed out by William Baumol, professor of economics at New York University and professor emeritus at Princeton, entrepreneurial efforts can be either productive or destructive, depending on the social and economic conditions in which entrepreneurs have to operate.[2]

Entrepreneurial efforts seek to focus on areas that provide the most promising returns. In this regard they are like water which flows naturally to where gravity draws it. So, entrepreneurs are by definition very adaptable. How they adapt to the environment, however, may create either productive results or destructive results from the perspective of the society and economic growth. Thus, under conditions of pervasive government regulations and intervention such as in the "license raj" of pre-reform India, entrepreneurs had to spend their efforts and resources to secure government permissions (licenses) for them to operate, and it often meant becoming a high-cost producer with a fixed market, thus rendering the market uncompetitive and inefficient.

In the former Soviet Union, successful entrepreneurs were those who could operate within the vast state bureaucracy to obtain preferential treatment or access to resources. While benefiting themselves and their partners in the bureaucracy, they made the bureaucratic apparatus even more sclerotic and inefficient. In other words, entrepreneurial efforts had become destructive from a society's point of view under such circumstances.

Asia's pragmatic and market-friendly economic policies, in contrast, have been able to channel entrepreneurial efforts in directions that not only benefit these entrepreneurs, but also the business environment and the economy as a whole.

Baumol identified several key conditions that are central to the kind of economic policies that can channel entrepreneurial efforts to create both private gains and greater social benefits. The first is the protection of private properties and intellectual property rights, which requires a rule of law and sanctity of contracts.[3] Secondly the market must be kept reasonably open to entry by small start-ups, which in turn means checking the power of monopolies and would-be monopolies. Thirdly, and following from the second, the market is kept competitive by making it easy for new business start-ups to challenge the incumbents. This approach in turn means preventing collusions between large established businesses and the government to limit competition.

As the Austrian economist Friedrich Hayek presciently pointed out, the proper role of the government in a market economy is first to make sure that it can control the governed through law and order; and, secondly and more importantly, that it can control itself.[4] Asia has by no means been completely successful in implementing economic policies that fully meet these conditions. But, by and large, the conditions outlined by Baumol have been embraced as principles in most Asian markets, even if they fall short in implementation and in details. Further, most Asian governments have managed to "control" themselves in the sense meant by Hayek, refraining from over-intrusive interference in the market.

Within this generally market-friendly environment, Asia's entrepreneurs have thrived in the last half a century. They have been instrumental in building dynamic businesses that transformed Asia. They made it possible for tens of millions of people to have regular and increasingly better paid employment, and to look forward to improving living conditions and life chances. The successful entrepreneurs of Asia have made themselves rich, and in so doing they have also made it possible for many others to become affluent. It is this segment of the consumer market, the affluent and the rich, that this book is about.

PATHWAYS TO AFFLUENCE

In the center of Georgetown on the island of Penang, off the west coast of Peninsula Malaysia, is a classical Chinese building known locally as the Blue Mansion because of its distinctive blue paint work. It was built in the 19th century, combining traditional Chinese architecture-in design, roofing, gold-gilding and porcelain mosaic—with Victorian cast ironworks and stained glass windows and panels imported from Glasgow, Scotland. It is now an exquisite heritage boutique hotel, lovingly restored and resplendent with its five courtyards and six wings of six rooms each, all arranged in harmony according to the principle of *feng shui* (geomancy). It was built by Chinese Malaysian businessman Cheong Fatt Tze, as the residence for his seventh and favorite wife.

Cheong arrived in British Malaya in 1856, from the southern Chinese province of Guandong; he was a penniless and illiterate teenager. He found work immediately as a water bearer and laborer. When he died in 1916, he was known as the "Rockefeller" of the East, having amassed a huge fortune from trading commodities and lucrative investments in banking, mining, plantations, textiles and cattle. He owned real estate and homes in China, Hong Kong, Singapore, Indonesia and Malaya. He was also a visionary—he introduced modern mining technology in his tin mines; launched a trans-Pacific shipping line between China and the US, and, after having developed a taste for European wines, built a winery in Shantung province in China in 1892 with imported grape vine-cuttings from Europe. A philanthropist, he donated generously to schools, hospitals, and religious institutions, and was always a leading donor in contributing to the region's disaster relief work. While maintaining his Chinese roots, he worked well with the British and Dutch colonial authorities, and educated his children in European schools so that they could represent him in the Western world.[5] When he died, British and Dutch authorities ordered flags to be lowered to half-mast in all official buildings in Hong Kong, British Malaya and Indonesia to honor him.

Cheong was the archetypal entrepreneur and business tycoon of Southeast Asia, albeit a fabulously successful one in his time. He was by no means unique. He was followed by later generations of Asian entrepreneurs—starting out with practically nothing and succeeding against the odds. He was, from a business perspective, an innovator par excellence. He globalized early in developing his empire, building business connections across the whole of Southeast and East Asia. He was pragmatic in working with the authorities, be they Chinese, British, Dutch or American. He was a traditionalist who could appreciate and exploit commercially nontraditional ideas. He was at once conservative and yet a risk-taker. And, above all, he was highly capable of adapting to the changing social, political and cultural environments of his time. This pattern lives on in Asia today and helps to define the specific pathway to affluence in Asia.

In postwar Asia, the social and political conditions were, of course, very different from Cheong's time. In war-ruined Japan for instance, the sense of cultural cohesion and national identity remained intact, and the foundation of industrialization assembled in the prewar era was there for a new generation of entrepreneurs to build on. But the situation was not the same in Southeast Asia where the struggle for political independence and new national identities was raging. Moreover, as mentioned earlier, the possibility of a market economy came to an end with the victory of the communists in mainland China; and the market economy was bundled into a straitjacket in India by Nehru socialism. In these two countries entrepreneurial drive was limited until recent times, which now define the pathways to affluence in these countries. These issues will be explored in the chapters following as we assess and evaluate the size and spending power of the affluent of Asia one key market at a time.

Against this general background of Asia's social and political conditions of the last 50 years, three distinct pathways to affluence can be defined. They are: (i) the pioneering pathway, (ii) the inheritance pathway and (iii) the professional pathway.

The pioneering pathway is the road taken by someone like Cheong Fatt Tze who created massive wealth from literally nothing, seizing on and exploiting opportunities seen only by him. While education opportunities have vastly improved in most of post-World War II Asia compared to Cheong's time, many entrepreneurs who have risen up through this pioneering pathway would not have been among the best educated. Many are from humble backgrounds and their history would still fit the rags-to-riches story. But there are also entrepreneurs who came from relatively well-off families, and launched themselves into new ventures without much family support and succeeded in spite of it. Their experiences could also be described as belonging to the pioneering pathway. By definition, the pioneering pathway is the road taken by the true originals, and hence always a minority of the affluent.

The inheritance pathway, on the other hand, refers to the experience of those who could pursue their dream of getting rich with some inherited wealth, family connections and support. Entrepreneurial ambitions, skills and luck are still important since inheritance is no guarantee of success. The difference between the inheritance and the pioneering pathways is, of course, the point of departure. There are, it must be said, both distinct advantages and disadvantages with the inheritance pathway. It certainly offers a better "endowed" starting point, be it a good education, some seed money, or connections in the right places; but it may also become a burden, cramping entrepreneurial ambitions and independence. For many, it is a double-edged sword.

Finally, there is the professional pathway to affluence. This refers to the path of acquiring professional skills and accreditations to allow the individual to enter well-paid employment with large corporations or as self-employed professionals. An advanced education is virtually a prerequisite for this pathway. Successful lawyers and doctors are the usual examples of self-employed professionals that can command high fees and, over a number of years, build up enough private assets to be among the affluent. Senior business executives are the others. When a society develops and its formal sector expands, as has been the case for most of Asia in the last 50 years, this professional pathway to affluence becomes more available to a larger number of people. The drawback of this pathway, however, is that it is a path of steady accumulation of modest wealth as opposed to dramatic breakthroughs into fabulous riches. The vast majority who rise up through this pathway will end up, as is defined in the next section, among the mass affluent and not the rich.

Before getting into the details of these different pathways to affluence in the contexts of specific markets, there is the matter of how to define the affluent.

DEFINING THE AFFLUENT

In the next seven chapters, the size of affluent consumers is systematically assessed and their spending power estimated in each market. These households are in turn aggregated into two segments—the "mass affluent" and the "rich." The defining income thresholds for "mass affluent" and "rich" are summarized in Table 1.5 below. For example in Australia, mass affluent households are defined as those earning $100,000 to $250,000 per year, whereas rich households are those earning above $250,000 a year. Japan, Hong Kong and Singapore share the same definitions.

In making cross-market comparisons, the effects of "purchasing power parity" (PPP) needs to be taken into account. This simply means that in different markets an equivalent unit of money (calculated based on the official exchange rates) could have very different purchasing power. PPP results from both the differences in the costs of similar goods and services, and, to a lesser extent, different levels of tax burden between markets. Thus, a haircut may cost the equivalent of $3 in Beijing and $45 in Tokyo, even after adjusting for the quality of service. Taking into account the effects of PPP, the income thresholds for affluent and rich households are therefore generally lower in lower income markets. In Korea and Taiwan, for example, the mass affluent households are accordingly defined as those earning $75,000 to $200,000, and rich households are those earning above $200,000 a year.

When one factors in the effects of PPP in markets such as Malaysia and Thailand, this lowers the income thresholds further for the mass affluent and rich households. In these two markets, the income thresholds for mass affluent and the rich households are $30,000 to $100,000 and above $100,000 a year respectively. In the Philippines the income thresholds are $15,000 to $75,000 and above $75,000 a year respectively for mass affluent and the rich households. In China and India, the income thresholds are lower still at $7,500 to $50,000, and above $50,000 a year for mass affluent and rich households, respectively. Table 1.5 summarizes these income thresholds.

Table 1.5
Income Definitions of "Mass Affluent" and "Rich" Households

Market	Income Level of Mass Affluent Households	Income Level of Rich Households
Australia	$100,000 - $250,000	$250,000+
China	$7,500 - $50,000	$50,000+
Hong Kong	$100,000 - $250,000	$250,000+
India	$7,500 - $50,000	$50,000+
Japan	$100,000 - $250,000	$250,000+
Korea	$75,000 - $200,000	$200,000+
Malaysia	$30,000 - $100,000	$100,000+
Philippines	$15,000 - $75,000	$75,000+
Singapore	$100,000 - $250,000	$250,000+
Taiwan	$75,000 - $200,000	$200,000+
Thailand	$30,000 - $100,000	$100,000+

(MasterCard Worldwide, Asia/Pacific)

In spite of these divergent income thresholds for defining the mass affluent and the rich in the different markets, they share common underlying characteristics as consumers, as will be explored in the following chapters.

JAPAN'S AFFLUENT CONSUMERS 2

The arrival of the 21ˢᵗ century seemed to coincide with a revival of Japan's economic fortunes. In the aftermath of the burst of the "bubble" economy in the early 1990s, the Japanese economy stagnated for over a decade. Sustained economic growth returned only in 2002/2003. The steady and relatively strong growth in private domestic consumption since 2003 is particularly encouraging.

Table 2.1

Revival of Economic Growth

	2001	2002	2003	2004	2005	2006*
Real GDP Growth	0.4%	0.1%	1.8%	2.3%	2.8%	3.4%
Growth of Private consumption	1.4%	1.1%	0.6%	1.9%	2.1%	3.6%

(Government of Japan; * 2006 estimates by MasterCard Asia/Pacific)

The "lost decade" of the 1990s, as it is commonly known, will likely go down in history as the third episode of Japan reinventing itself economically in the past 150 years. The first is the Meiji Restoration in 1868, and the second is the post-World War II reconstruction. In each of these earlier episodes, existing economic power and hierarchies were either destroyed or significantly reduced, and new avenues of social and economic mobility opened up along with robust economic growth.

The Meiji Restoration, which toppled the rule of the shogun (the military strongmen that ruled in the name of the emperor), also eliminated the privileged position held by the samurai, the hereditary warrior class. In their place came entrepreneurs, who in the period between the Meiji Restoration and the end of World War II created a new kind of business: the massive family-controlled industrial conglomerates, known as *zaibatsu* (which literally means a "wealthy clique"). These conglomerates encompassed heavy industries, light industries, construction, transportation, finance and consumer durables. Many famous names in Japanese business today came from the *zaibatsu* of that era—Mitsubishi, Mitsui, Sumitomo, Nomura and Nissan, to name a few. These families amassed fabulous wealth in a matter of decades.

These *zaibatsu* were chiefly responsible for importing technologies and expertise from the industrial powers of Europe and the US in the second half of the 19th century and early 20th century. Many operated with direct government sponsorship. They created an industrial working class for the first time in Japan, absorbing tens and thousands of rural-urban migrants into their factories. And, as it transpired, Japan's single-minded determination to achieve rapid industrialization was closely intertwined with its development of a modern military—the building of an army based on the Prussian model, and a navy in the mold of the Royal Navy of Great Britain. The *zaibatsu*, having created the industrial infrastructure, also became arms manufacturers and virtual partners of the government in Japan's aggressive pre-World War II militarization.[1]

After World War II, many *zaibatsu* were slated to be broken up by the Allies. Many survived, however, albeit with scaled-down operations, and with some losing their former quasi-monopoly positions. This shift cleared the field for a new generation of entrepreneurs to emerge. A case in point is how Taikichiro Mori got started. He was the founder of one of Japan's most successful property companies, Mori Building. A business professor from Yokohama, Mori was struck by how cheap land was in Tokyo in the early 1950s against its pre-war values. So he began buying lots in desirable parts of Tokyo, starting in the Minato ward in central Tokyo, a neighborhood that he knew well because his family had been there for generations working as tobacconists and rice merchants. By the time he died in 1993, Mori Building was one of the biggest property companies in Japan, and Mori himself was named twice, in 1991 and 1992, as the richest man in the world by *Forbes* magazine (his fortune no doubt boosted by the "bubble" economy just before his death).[2] With the *zaibatsu* seriously weakened and in disarray, it became easier for entrepreneurs without government connections or massive financial backing, such as Mori, to capture business opportunities.

In postwar Japan the government gradually took control of the commanding heights of the economy formerly controlled by the *zaibatsu* families. Powerful government ministries, such as the Ministry of International Trade and Industry (MITI), used "administrative guidance" to influence industrial development. A second development was the keiretsu system, which replaced the pre-war *zaibatsu*.

The *keiretsu* (literally meaning a "series") were essentially networks of banks and companies structured around a set of horizontal relationships between members. The bank often acted as the leader of the *keiretsu*, being the lender of business loans to other *keiretsu* members. Many members were suppliers to and buyers from each other. The relationships were solidified by cross-shareholding of members. Through this structure, the government could "guide" businesses to focus on what MITI saw as priority industries and markets; and nudge the banks, should they need to be nudged, to lend to businesses that were moving in the "guided" direction. How the government regulated industries became indistinguishable from how they promoted them.

The *keiretsu* system was clearly much less stifling than the pre-war *zaibatsu*; market competition could often be intense, and it was possible, though difficult, for small new business entrants to emerge to challenge dominant incumbents. The best of the entrepreneurs, like Akio Morita who founded Sony, could build a world-class business from scratch in the shadows of big incumbent conglomerates. Morita, after all, started Sony in a small workshop and had no privileged connections to any *keiretsu*.

THE PROFESSIONAL PATHWAY TO AFFLUENCE

This system worked extremely well for the next four decades. By the early 1970s, Japan's GDP had been growing at an average of some 9.5% per year for 25 years, allowing per capita income to reach that of Western Europe. Japanese brands came to dominate markets such as consumer electronics, motorcycles and low-end automobiles. Just as the *zaibatsu* had created Japan's first industrial working class, the *keiretsu* created a massive middle class of white collar workers—the "salaryman." Secured by an implicit social contract of lifetime employment, the middle class spent judiciously within their means, and saved diligently, while gradually improving their living standards. In the 1960s, they focused on acquiring the "three treasures" of television, washing machine and refrigerator. In 1970s, they moved on to acquire the three "Cs"—car, color television and air conditioner.

The expanding middle class constituted a receptive market for the growth of well paid professional services. These services included doctors, lawyers and accountants. The professional pathway to affluence now started to function in earnest, as professionals and senior business executives steadily increased their earnings, and joined the ranks of the mass affluent, and occasionally, the rich. From a purely numerical point of view, this pathway was perhaps the most important for the vast majority of Japan's middle class to achieve affluence status.

THE INHERITANCE PATHWAY TO AFFLUENCE

The inheritance pathway, on the other hand, was also functioning well as second- and third-generations of wealthy families entered into businesses, often using the family enterprise only as a platform for new ventures, and frequently reinventing the family concern to adapt to new environments. Some of the lineage of the inheritance goes back a long way, such as the family-owned beverage business Suntory.

Shinjiro Torii founded the company in 1899 in Osaka to make Japan's first domestic wine and liquor. Trying to make western wine and liquor in a tradition-bound country that up to then only drank *sake* (rice wine) was a pioneering entrepreneurial plunge if there ever was one. The company ventured into whisky production in 1923, carefully calibrating the taste (making it lighter) to suit the Japanese. Torii was rewarded with the successful launch of Suntory White whisky, followed by the now famous Suntory Old whisky, which quickly captured wide sales in Japan. Shinjiro Torii died in 1962 aged 83, a highly successful and respected business patriarch. His second son, Keizo, joined the company in 1945 and became president in 1961, a year before his father's death.

Keizo expanded the company's offerings to include beer, restaurants and biotechnology products. Keizo died in 1999 aged 80, and the management of Suntory was passed onto his nephew

Shinichiro Torii, the founder's grandson. Nobutada Saji took over from Shinichiro in 2001 (Saji is also descended from the founder Torii despite his different last name). In recent years Suntory has moved into yet another new business—pharmaceuticals, leveraging on its biotechnology knowledge base of working with plants and herbs, and focusing on immunology as well as on treating problems in the cardiovascular system and the central nervous system. Thus, Suntory remains a highly innovative company even as it is now being managed by the third generation of its founding family.[3]

The inheritance pathway has, however, sometimes led to the second generation splitting up the business, often acrimoniously. An example is Mori Building mentioned earlier. When the founder Taikichiro Mori died in 1993, his two sons, Minoru and Akira, came into conflict over their different visions of how the business should be run and developed. This resulted in the business being split into two; Minoru runs Mori Building with sales of $1.3 billion and 122 buildings under management, and Akira runs the Mori Trust with sales of $950 million and 68 buildings under management. In the next decade, Minoru and Akira took their respective businesses into opposite directions. Minoru is a visionary who thinks and dreams big, whereas Akira is a cautious conservative. And, in spite of their rivalry, both have been successful in their own ways.

Minoru's vision is nothing less than changing how the Japanese live. Central to his vision is the creation of a living environment that eliminates the typical two- to three-hour-long daily commute that most Tokyo residents face and frees them up to have more leisure time. An embodiment of his vision is his Roppongi Hills project opened in downtown Tokyo in 2003. It featured a 54-story office tower and 793 apartments, all integrated with shops, restaurants, parks and gardens, and movie theatres. A showcase feature is the Mori Art Museum, occupying a trophy location on the 52nd and 53rd floors of the office tower. It is meant to be a total working and living environment. Some observers now believe that Minoru's vision could very well be an accurate foretaste of things to come; Japan's rapidly increasing elderly population, many of whom are in the mass affluent category, seem to prefer to live in an urban environment with well-integrated functional and recreational space. Minoru's vision is not limited to Japan. He is actively pursuing projects overseas, including the plan to build the world's tallest building in Shanghai.[4]

Akira's vision, in contrast, is much more conservative, both in strategic and financial terms. He sees himself more as a custodian of assets instead of an agent of change. He has steadily increased his real estate holdings and properties under management, selecting those with strong cash flow, solid brands and good track records. His newly opened Conrad Tokyo is a case in point. While Minoru's grand projects often put him in financial difficulties, Akira's personal fortune has been rising inexorably. In fact, he was ranked by *Forbes* as Japan's fifth richest man in 2006, with an estimated net worth of $4.9 billion.[5] Minoru did not make the list.

THE PIONEERING PATHWAY TO AFFLUENCE

Fabulous paper wealth was created for not only the rich, but for virtually every owner of urban property in Japan during the "bubble" economy. By the end of the 1980s, the height of the "bubble" economy, the capitalization of the Tokyo Stock Exchange was equal to that of the New York Stock Exchange. And, of the world's 10 largest banks, eight were Japanese.

Like all bubbles, the one in Japan duly burst and the economy went into a prolonged stagnation through the 1990s and early 2000s. Future historians may well look back at this period as Japan's third episode of economic reinvention. Many signs are still tentative, but the outline of a new pattern is becoming discernable. The business environment is becoming more open and competitive. Social pressure to conform to the status quo appears to have lessened.

MITI no longer has a grip on "guiding" Japan's economic and business development strategies. Financial institutions, including the gigantic banking groups that emerged from the consolidation of the sector, are now turning their attention to consumers and small businesses, entirely new sets of customers very different from their large corporate borrowers of the past. In this third episode of Japan's economic reinvention, the circle may finally be completed—the time for pioneering entrepreneurs may be arriving, just as it did after the Meiji Restoration 138 years ago.

There is no better example than Masayoshi Son. Often referred to as Japan's answer to Bill Gates, Son was born in 1958 in Tosu City on the southern island of Kyushu, to parents of second-generation Korean immigrants. His father ran a *pachinko* parlor (Japan's ubiquitous pinball machine arcade) and had the financial means to send Son to high school and then university in California. Returning to Japan, Son, a computer wiz and true to his entrepreneurial calling, forsook the career path of a salaryman with a big corporation, and started Softbank in 1981 as a software distributor.

In the next 10 years, Son gradually built up Softbank to become Japan's largest wholesaler of computer software, systems and peripherals. The coming of the internet was custom-made for an entrepreneur like Son. He was in his element. He took Softbank public with a successful IPO in 1994, then launched the company into the new business of hosting computer trade shows, and publishing computer magazines by buying titles such as *PC Magazine*, *PC Week* and *PC Computing*. His next big move was to team up with Rupert Murdoch's News Corp. to buy into Japan's television network of TV Asahi, and then in a series of dissolving and forming new partnerships with the likes of Sony Corp. and Fuji Television, he launched SkyPerfecTV in 1998, offering subscribers more than 150 channels. By 2000, Son's competitor, DirecTV, succumbed and agreed to a merger with SkyPerfecTV. All in all it was an extraordinary series of successful deal-making riding on the internet boom.

With the internet on his mind, Son went into consumer finance as well, taking on Japan's banking giants. Softbank started to offer services in online banking, investment advice, broking, insurance and consumer credit. He partnered with US-based Nasdaq to create Nasdaq Japan. And, in 2000, he bought the failed Nippon Credit Bank for $1 billion.[6] Son survived the dotcom bust and went into the mobile phone business and expanded into Korea, China and the US. In 2006, his internet phone and ADSL service has more than five million subscribers in Japan, and he recently purchased Vodafone's Japan operations for $17 billion. With a personal net worth of $7 billion, Son ranked number one on *Forbes'* list of Japan's richest in 2006.

Son's meteoric rise to become the richest man in Japan is indicative of the arrival of a new business environment in the country in more ways than one. Ethnically Korean, Son had certainly been an outsider as far as corporate Japan was concerned. He was never a part of any *keiretsu*, and has never joined one. His education was American, hence he did not have the old-school ties and connections so essential to a successful business career in the old mold. He made his entry into business riding on a new technology, and then continued to ride the subsequent technological waves to stay at the forefront of change. He started partnering with foreign businesses early, bringing them into notoriously insular Japan. His success is therefore a product of his ambitions and skills as much as the rapidly changing social, technological and business environments. This combination is an intoxicating mix, which is setting a new foundation for the pioneering pathway to affluence to kick into high gear in the coming decade.

The pattern of how the three pathways to affluence have worked since the Meiji Restoration is illustrated in Chart 2.1.

Chart 2.1

Japan's Pathway to Affluence

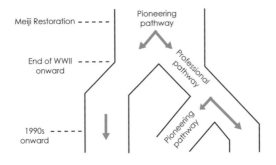

The opening up (once again) of Japan's pioneering pathway to affluence can be illustrated by the changing composition of the richest families in terms of their business sectors between 1996 and 2005. Chart 2.2 shows the composition by their business sectors of the top 27 richest Japanese families, each with more than $1 billion of assets in 1996. Manufacturing was the biggest sector, accounting for 24% of the richest families. This was followed by real estate, accounting for 22%. Finance was in the third place with 14%. Leisure and food and beverage tied for fourth place with 8% each. IT occupied the fifth place with only 5%.

Chart 2.2

Industry Sectors of top 27 richest families with over $1 billion assets in Japan (1996)

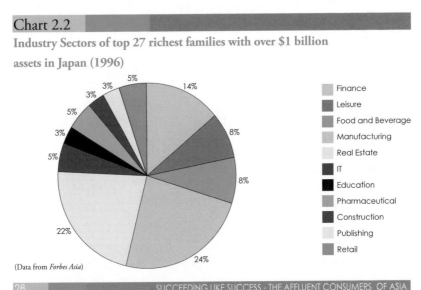

(Data from *Forbes Asia*)

By 2005, the picture looked very different. The share of the richest families in manufacturing had shrunk from 24% to 16%, and real estate from 22% to 16%. Finance's share rose to 28% to become the number one sector. This clearly reflects massive new business opportunities created in personal and consumer finance in the years between 1996 and 2005. Leisure's share of the richest families rose to 20% to become the number two sector, again heralding significant lifestyle changes. IT rose from the minuscule 5% in 1996 to account for 12% of Japan's richest families, ranking as the number four sector.

Chart 2.3

Industry Sectors of top 27 richest families with over $1 billion assets in Japan (2005)

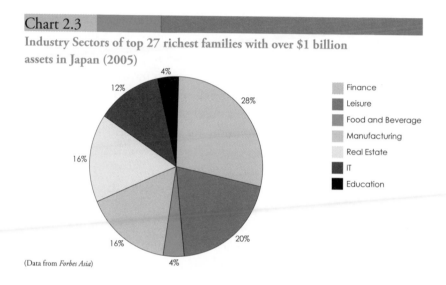

Finance
Leisure
Food and Beverage
Manufacturing
Real Estate
IT
Education

(Data from *Forbes Asia*)

With hindsight, it is quite apparent that the pioneering pathway to affluence in Japan had been compromised by the stable and secure employment conditions created by corporate Japan in the postwar decades, especially the practice of lifetime employment. For at least two, if not three, generations, most of the best and brightest, and the best educated, were lured to climb the corporate ladder. The professional pathway to affluence became the preferred option for the vast majority. The result was, to borrow J.K. Galbraith's famous phrase, "the bland leading the bland."

The system was not without its benefits, witness the large middle class with an enviable record of equitable income distribution.

It was a highly stable social structure that enjoyed steady growth shared by many. But it sapped Japan's entrepreneurial energy and cramped the style of the maverick, if not holding them back altogether. Epitomized by Masayoshi Son, Japan's entrepreneurial spirit is again on the rise, and the pioneering pathway to affluence will likely be turned into a highway in the coming years.

SIZE AND SPENDING POWER OF THE MASS AFFLUENT AND THE RICH

The total number of households that belonged to the mass affluent category in 2005 was estimated at 4.8 million, which accounted for 9.5% of Japan's total households. Assuming a trend rate of real GDP growth of 2% in the next decade, their number is expected to grow by about 4.9% per year to reach over 7 million in 2015, and will account for 12.9% of total households as shown in Table 2.2. The mass affluent therefore accounts for a significant portion of the total households in Japan. It is a unique feature of Japan.

The total income of the mass affluent households was estimated at $613.6 billion in 2005, and is projected to grow by 5.1% per year, assuming a trend rate of real GDP growth of 2% per year in the next decade. This trend will bring their total income to $923.4 billion in 2015. Their average household income was $129,000 in 2005, and will be virtually unchanged at $130,000 in 2015.

Table 2.2

Size and Income of the Mass Affluent

Annual income $100,000 to $250,000 (2004 US$ & exchange rate)	2005	2015	Cumulative annual growth
Number of Households	4.8 million	7.1 million	4.9%
Total Household Income	$613.6 billion	$923.4 billion	5.1%
Average Annual Household Income	$129,000	$130,000	0.1%

(MasterCard Worldwide, Asia/Pacific)

The number of households that qualify for the rich category was estimated at 554,000 in 2005, and they accounted for 1.1% of total households. By 2015, it is expected that the number of rich households will rise to close to one million, and they will account for about 1.8% of Japan's total households.

Total household income of the rich households in Japan was estimated at $192.5 billion in 2005, and is projected to grow quite fast by 7.8% per year to reach $341.8 billion in 2015. Their average household income in 2005 was $348,000, which will increase only very slowly by about 0.2% per year to $353,000 in 2015. The overall pattern is that while the numbers of the mass affluent and rich households are expected to increase quite fast in the next 10 years at 4.9% and 5.7% per year, their average household income will remain almost unchanged in real terms.

Table 2.3

Size and Income of the Rich

Annual income $250,000+ (constant 2004 US$)	2005	2015	Cumulative annual growth
Number of Households	554,000	967,000	5.7%
Total Household Income	$192.5 billion	$341.8 billion	7.8%
Average Annual Household Income	$348,000	$353,000	0.2%

(MasterCard Worldwide, Asia/Pacific)

The discretionary spending on a per household basis is estimated at $24,800 and $66,800 for the mass affluent and the rich, respectively in 2005. By 2015, they are projected to increase to $31,200 and $84,700, respectively. Given their high average incomes, these levels of discretionary spending are relatively low, reflecting Japan's household propensities to save as well as the high costs of living, even for basic necessities.

Table 2.4

Discretionary Spending Estimates

Per Household Discretionary Spending (constant 2004 US$)	2005	2015	Cumulative annual growth
The Mass Affluent	$24,800	$31,200	2.3%
The Rich	$66,800	$84,700	2.4%

(MasterCard Worldwide, Asia/Pacific)

The mass affluent spend most on dining and entertaining, and on travel and related leisure activities. These two items accounted for 32.5% and 29.7% of their total discretionary spending respectively in 2005. This was followed by shopping, then spending on automobiles, PCs and mobile phones. This pattern is expected to remain the same in 2015.

Table 2.5

Key Discretionary Expenditure of the Mass Affluent

Key discretionary Expenditure Items (2004 US$ billion)	2005	2015	Cumulative annual growth
Dining and Entertaining	$38.3	$54.4	4.2%
Shopping	$19.5	$29.0	5.0%
Travel & Leisure	$35.0	$50.1	4.6%
Private Health & Luxury Medicine	$6.3	$9.0	4.4%
Automobiles, PCs & Mobile Phones, etc.	$18.9	$27.1	4.4%
Total	$118.0	$169.1	4.5%

(MasterCard Worldwide, Asia/Pacific)

For rich households, discretionary spending on dining and entertaining, and on travel and related leisure activities are also the two largest expenditures. Compared with the mass affluent households, the growth rates on all discretionary expenditure items for rich households are expected to be higher, in the 7% per year range.

Table 2.6

Key Discretionary Expenditure of the Rich

Key discretionary Expenditure Items (2004 US$ billion)	2005	2015	Cumulative annual growth
Dining and Entertaining	$12.0	$20.1	6.8%
Shopping	$6.1	$10.8	7.6%
Travel & Leisure	$11.0	$18.9	7.2%
Private Health & Luxury Medicine	$2.0	$3.3	7.0%
Automobiles, PCs & Mobile Phones, etc.	$5.9	$10.0	7.0%
Total	$37.0	$63.1	7.1%

(MasterCard Worldwide, Asia/Pacific)

The pathways to affluence through which these premium consumers, in both the mass affluent and the rich categories, have arrived at their income levels are of central significance, and are expected to have a decisive influence, especially from the point of view of their value perceptions and behavior as consumers.

THE PROFESSIONAL PATHWAY TO AFFLUENCE

This pathway is likely to be the most common among the mass affluent households. Many of these households will reach retirement age in the next 10 years.[7] Many will be in the empty nesters and old singles life stages. Thus, their lifelong conservative and frugal habits are unlikely to change. These cautious consumers will remain keen to get value for money.

THE INHERITANCE PATHWAY TO AFFLUENCE

In the next 10 years, a surprising number of the mass affluent and rich households will come through the inheritance pathway due to the sheer effect of legacy that the elderly will leave behind. It has been estimated that about 70% of all privately held assets, including real estate assets, belong to those aged 50 and above. In the past 10 years, the average amount of inheritance left by the elderly of Japan was estimated at around $330,000, a very sizable sum.[8]

A potentially very interesting development is the convergence of the inheritance and the pioneering pathways when the inheritance is being used to launch business ventures and innovative projects by those inheriting the assets. As the social and business conditions are improving for new business start-ups, such a convergence could produce a dynamic new generation of successful entrepreneurs.

To the extent that this potential can be realized, the inheritance pathway will create a segment of the premium consumers in the mass affluent and rich households that are younger, less risk aversive and more experimental.

THE PIONEERING PATHWAY TO AFFLUENCE

The premium consumers that will come through this pathway in the next 10 years in Japan are very likely to be the most dynamic, individually minded and non-conventional consumers that the country has ever seen. As argued above, this pathway to affluence will be working overtime in the coming years as the social and business environments are changing fast, becoming more supportive and conducive to entrepreneurial efforts. Many of the successful entrepreneurs will jump directly to the rich-household category, bypassing the mass affluence stage. They will be high-power, trendsetting, as well as demanding premium consumers.

Together the mass affluent and the rich households of Japan will command $230 billion of discretionary spending in 2015, a sum that is larger than the GDP of many countries in Asia and elsewhere. This is a market that is at once high end, massive and diversified; in other words, full of exciting business opportunities.

CHINA'S AFFLUENT
CONSUMERS 3

In April 2006, Shanghai hosted Asia's first Millionaire Fair. This annual exhibition, which started in Europe in 2001, showcases luxury goods from upscale villas to yachts to diamond tiaras to private islands. Some 10,000 VIP guests, multimillionaires from all over China, attended. Amid gala dinners and cocktail receptions, the rich and famous, as well as the rich and not yet famous, mingled and networked.

The organizers were quick to point out the significance of choosing Shanghai for their first event in Asia; the city is the most exciting and dynamic growth hub in China where new millionaires are being minted at a fast and furious pace.[1] In 2005, the Chinese Academy of Social Sciences estimated that there were 10,000 entrepreneurs with net assets of over $10 million each, and some 300,000 with an individual net worth exceeding $1 million.[2] A new "long march" to be rich and famous is well underway in China. It has, of course, not always been like that.

Upon taking power on the mainland of China in 1949, Mao Zedong and his communist comrades embarked on what they saw as their epic historical task of transforming China. Among the several "enemies of the people" that they wanted to obliterate from the face of China was the bourgeoisie, owners and operators of private businesses. Nationalization of private businesses ensued, and by the mid-1950s private businesses had, even in small-scale retail and related industries, completely disappeared in urban China. In rural China, communes had replaced private land holdings. The bourgeoisie had indeed been wiped clean from the surface of China.

What followed in the period leading up to the 1978 economic reform and market opening, scarred by the 10 years of turmoil and upheaval of the Cultural Revolution (1966-1976), can only be described as a process of destruction of old wealth and resolute suppression of the creation of new private wealth. The next period, from 1978 to the early 1990s, can be seen as a transitional time. Market opening, which started in tentative and small steps, slowly gained traction and momentum. Reform started in the rural sector first, allowing peasants to privately cultivate and sell farm produce, freeing them from the yoke of the communes. Farm productivity quadrupled in the next decade as a result and it basically solved the problem of China's food supply. Rural reform took a big step forward when the peasants were granted a 30-year lease on their land, a step closer to outright private land ownership.

The emergence of the private sector in urban China started in earnest only in the late 1990s, after China secured World Trade Organization admission. The scaling back of the state sector in the 1990s, especially of businesses run by local governments and the military, gradually opened the way for a whole new generation of private entrepreneurs to enter the market. The lifting of government control of most prices gave entrepreneurs better signals on how to invest and what to produce. Fragmented local markets were slowly consolidated and an embryonic national market began to emerge. All these were critical factors that assisted the effectiveness of entrepreneurial efforts in China. Realizing how important private entrepreneurs were for job creation to mitigate the massive layoffs in the state sector, the central government granted constitutional recognition to private sector business owners in 1999. Now China has come full circle—the bourgeoisie are back.

The generations of Chinese that came of age over the last half century have been deeply affected by massive social and economic upheavals. Many were touched by famines and other disasters, manmade as well as natural. Their personal experiences also differed greatly from one generation to the next. From this perspective, there are four broadly defined generations: (i) the "founding generation" of those who are 70 years and older; (ii) the Cultural Revolution generation who are between 50 and 65 years old; (iii) the upwardly mobile generation who are 30 to 49 years old, and (iv) the "young emperor" generation of those who are 29 and under.

The founding generation was at least 40 years old when reform and market opening started, and most of them would have missed the boat of the new opportunities offered. Many of them have neither the skills nor the motivation to take the plunge into the embryonic market economy. For the Cultural Revolution generation, however, the situation was quite different. For the lucky ones who could continue their interrupted education or who had the contacts and resources to go into business, the decades of the 1980s and 1990s represented undreamt of opportunities after the nightmarish years of the Cultural Revolution. Ironically, their experiences in the chaos and violence of the 1970s would have toughened some of them and rendered them less risk-averse. Many of China's entrepreneurial pioneers came from this generation.

Members of the upwardly mobile generation, the oldest of whom were only in their early 20s when reform started, are the prime beneficiaries. At minimum, the impact of the reform has been that most of them became better educated than the previous generation. Better education meant not only being able to finish high school and even attending university, but more importantly, being able to learn skills relevant to the emerging market economy. Today, the "vintage" of education is a key indicator of how useful a person's education is as a "door opener" toward better paid and professional employment.

Finally, the "young emperor" generation refers to those born after market reform had started and, more significantly, after the "One Child" policy was introduced. They were literally born in an entirely new era, and in a family context where a single child is the norm. As parents doted on their single child, assisted enthusiastically by the grandparents, the single child grew up spoiled as no children in China had for generations. Dubbed the "young emperors," they are the best educated, most confident and ambitious among all the living generations in China today. Often self-centered and frequently self-indulgent, they are also the most avid and savvy consumers.

With the exception of the "founding generation," the other three generations clearly have embraced the market economy and pursued all available avenues for self-advancement. For these three generations the earlier revolutionary zest for collective prosperity and socialist equality has vanished and been replaced by a new quest for personal affluence. The three pathways to affluence are in good operating order in China today, albeit with uniquely Chinese characteristics.

THE PROFESSIONAL PATHWAY TO AFFLUENCE

The professional pathway to affluence started to operate in China only with the arrival of foreign multinational companies in the 1980s. Foreign businesses, including those from Hong Kong, created a market for skilled business professionals, and they paid competitive market wages, which were typically a high multiple of what the same person could earn working for a government-run enterprise.

Such professional employment in turn stimulated the supply side-Chinese institutions of higher learning started to develop their capability to meet the demand for graduates in business administration, finance, marketing, IT and other sectors. Even before Chinese educational institutions started to respond to the new demand, enterprising Chinese students took to studying overseas. Between 1978 and 2005, it is estimated that some 900,000 Chinese students went overseas for higher education. It has been estimated that about 500,000 have returned, mostly since 1999.

These returnees have found a very dynamic and fast growing job market awaiting them. By the 1990s, the need for well trained and English-proficient business managers was not limited to foreign multinational companies. More and more Chinese companies, both state-owned and private, have started to introduce modern management techniques and import business know-how, in order to compete more effectively in the domestic market as well as preparing themselves for overseas competition. It was, and has continued to be, an environment ripe for the young and well trained to pursue a corporate career in a fast moving market.

China's educational institutions responded quickly to the new demand. Take the development of the Master of Business Administration (MBA) program, for example. In 1991, there were only nine universities officially approved to offer an MBA degree in China. A grand total of 86 MBA students graduated that year. By 2004, there were 89 universities officially approved to offer MBA degrees, and over 10,000 students graduating with MBAs that year. Cumulatively, it is estimated that there are about 90,000 homegrown MBA graduates in China today, an impressive record of rapid growth.

Needless to say, it is the "young emperor" generation, and to a lesser extent, the upwardly mobile generation, that have taken advantage of the professional pathway to affluence. Increasingly, however, this professional pathway is cross-fertilizing with the pioneering pathway to produce a whole new generation of young successful entrepreneurs. Many business school graduates opt to launch their own start-ups after working for a few years for a large company, often a multinational. With their technical training at school combined with hands-on learning in a large corporation, they have proved to be just as entrepreneurial as their pioneering elders, but clearly more sophisticated and better prepared.

THE PIONEERING PATHWAY TO AFFLUENCE

One of the truly amazing phenomena of contemporary China is that during half a century of socialism, with repeated and violent campaigns against capitalism and the bourgeoisie, the spirit of private entrepreneurship managed to stay alive. As hard as Mao tried, and as much as he believed that he had succeeded, the belief in private enterprise somehow could not be eradicated in China. As soon as the opportunity presented itself, it then became evident that beneath every drab Mao suit lurked a would-be capitalist ready to don his or her business suit. Even more surprising is the fact that the belief in private enterprise is alive and well not only among the young, but is also readily found among those who had suffered grievously through the Cultural Revolution.

An example of an entrepreneur, belonging to the Cultural Revolution generation, who took advantage of opportunities offered by economic reform to become a successful businessman is Liu Zhifang in Beijing. Born in 1956 in a village outside of Beijing, he had his education interrupted by the Cultural Revolution, and he went to a technical school instead of a high school. He remembers his youth as a period of great deprivation. After completing his trade school, he joined a state-owned construction company. Up to then Liu's life was typical of that of tens of millions of young Chinese of his generation: an interrupted education and a job in a government agency with limited prospects.

In 1979, one year after Deng Xiaoping's announcement of the "four modernizations" program that opened up the Chinese economy, Liu felt the winds of change. Many others no doubt felt the same, but Liu acted on his instincts. Aged 23, he took the plunge—quitting his government job and forsaking its security and regular income (an "iron rice bowl," however dull, dreary and lowly paid) and set up his own construction business—a classic risk-taking decision that is the trademark of a true entrepreneur.

He did not have much capital and it was tough going for a while. Then he had his first break. An Air Force agency wanted to have an old chimney pulled down in one of their buildings. Liu was contacted, possibly through some old connections from his government job days, and he offered to do the job in one day for 3,000 yuan ($375). He recalls that he did not earn any profit from the job after paying for the casual workers and the equipment rental. But he did the job on time and the Air Force agency was impressed. He was then signed up for a bigger project that was worth 400,000 yuan ($50,000), a huge sum in China in those days. Profits from that project gave him the break—he bought better equipment and hired more staff and then took on bigger and more profitable projects, and so things continued.

In 1983, Liu merged his company with a military business. At that time the military was heavily into running its own enterprises, and, again, Liu saw an opportunity to grow fast with connections brought by his military business partner. His joint venture company specialized in heavy earth-moving tasks in large construction projects because of their competitive advantage of having better equipment. Liu did not stand still. In 1990 he visited the US and made a careful study of the construction business there. He came away convinced that he needed better equipment and technology, and in the next few years he purchased the most advanced construction equipment from Japan and Germany. This move put him in a huge competitively advantageous position when the residential construction boom took off in the late 1990s.

Liu's passage to prosperity is typical of many successful Chinese entrepreneurs of his generation—toughened by having suffered through the Cultural Revolution and taking the plunge into the private sector with no formal training, they are nevertheless able to leverage old government connections to build a business while learning on the job and riding the wave of economic growth. In Liu's case, his success included attracting unwanted attention. He was kidnapped for ransom in 1995, beaten and locked up for a day before he was dumped by his kidnappers on a highway outside of Beijing.[3]

In contrast with Liu, Jason Jiang comes from the upwardly mobile generation (at the younger end of the age range) and built his wealth in a completely different way. At 33, he is estimated to have amassed a personal fortune of over $700 million. The company he founded in 2003, Focus Media, which he listed on Nasdaq in summer of 2005, has a market capitalization of $2.9 billion. Jiang made his fortune in a business that simply did not exist 10 years ago in China—advertising in the mass consumer market.

A Shanghai native, Jiang grew up as a single child in a modern (in China's context) middle class background; his father was an accountant and his mother a manager in the state-run grocery store. He attended college after high school, studying to be a teacher, and it was as a college student that he discovered his true talents. In need of pocket money, he worked part time selling print ads for an advertising company, and swiftly rose to become the top salesman while still trying to finish his studies. Having grown up with computers and the internet, he naturally gravitated to working with internet advertisers as well.

Giving up the idea of becoming a teacher upon graduation, Jiang founded Focus Media with seed money from Softbank China Venture Capital. In the "get rich is glorious" new China, Jiang knows that most affluent consumers spend more time outside of their home than in. Focus Media started selling advertising on a network of electronic billboards installed at elevator lobbies in office buildings in the large cities. Then Jiang quickly moved to establish franchises in the rising secondary cities as well when growth moved inland from the coastal region. As Focus Media's revenue grew, the company attracted new and weightier investors. Goldman Sachs, United China Investment and the 3i Group invested in Focus Media in 2004, and it listed in 2005.[4] Today, Jiang is a celebrity in China, and an inspiration to many young entrepreneurs. The Shanghai Municipal Government proudly lists him on its website as one of the "Top 10 Young Spirits of Shanghai."

The trajectories represented by Liu and Jiang, both pioneering entrepreneurs in their separate ways, are indicative of the dynamics embedded in the generational differences in China's entrepreneurial pathway to affluence. Growing up in different decades could mean huge gaps in education, management know-how and business skills. It is not surprising that Liu succeeds in construction while Jiang excels in advertising. How they negotiated their ways successfully through the pioneering pathway to affluence is a direct reflection of differences in their generational backgrounds.

Private entrepreneurs are transforming China, make no mistake about it. However, they still need to tread carefully, and demonstrate their contributions to China's development wherever they can. Zhang Yue, the founder of Broad Ltd., a Changsha-based maker of giant cooling systems that has successfully marketed its products worldwide, conspicuously displays in his office certificates attesting to Broad Ltd.'s having paid more taxes than any other private company. Not far from his office is the building that houses his private helicopter and jet.[5] This juxtaposition of certificates and private aircraft is highly symbolic of how Chinese entrepreneurs have chosen to travel on the pioneering pathway to affluence today.

THE INHERITANCE PATHWAY TO AFFLUENCE

Given the total destruction of private wealth in China under Mao, one may well ask: is there anything left to be inherited? As it happens, the answer is "quite a lot." And it has to do with the "princelings" phenomenon.

Children of the top leaders and high officials in China are known as "princelings." Before the 1980s, most princelings were given priority in terms of schooling, and many ended up being groomed for high positions within the government. Starting in the 1980s, and a powerful sign of change itself, many princelings opted to go into business instead of government. It is through their personal connections and family pedigrees that these princelings can be said to be able to pursue the inheritance pathway to affluence.

A high-profile princeling is Li Xiaolin, chief executive of China Power International Development Ltd., one of China's largest independent power companies. She is the daughter of former premier Li Peng, the prime advocate of the Three Gorges Dam on the Yangtze River and infamously associated with the violent crushing of student protest in the Tiananmen Square in 1989.

After graduating with a master's degree in engineering from the prestigious Tsinghua University, Li went abroad for further training, and attended the Sloan School of Management at MIT. Li's "inheritance" thus began with an Ivy League education that is simply not available to the vast majority of Chinese students, however talented they may be. Early exposure to how government and government-run business work is another part of her "inheritance." She remembers well the different inspection tours on which she went along with her father, visiting different power plants and industrial projects undertaken by the government, and meeting many senior officials and technocrats.

In 1994, when her father was prime minister of China, Li was chosen to join a newly formed company that eventually became China Power International Development. Li swiftly rose to the top and led the company to a public listing on the Hong Kong Stock Exchange in 2004, which proved to be a smashing success-it was oversubscribed 300 times and its share prices jumped 17% in the first day of trading.[6] There is no mistake about Li's family background and perceptions by the market of the company that she runs. Her pedigree is seen, rightly or wrongly, as an implicit guarantee that the company enjoys easy access to top government decision makers and can be trusted to be well-informed on important policies and even on what senior government officials may be thinking.

Other top level princelings who have gone into high profile corporate positions include Jiang Mianheng, son of former president Jiang Zemin. Jiang Mianheng sits on the boards of a number of high-tech companies, in addition to being the vice president of the Chinese Academy of Sciences. Former Premier Zhu Rongji's son, Levin Zhu Yunlai, is the CEO of China International Capital Corp., an investment bank that counts Morgan Stanley as one of its shareholders. Wang Jun, son of late vice president Wang Zhen, now heads the China CITIC Group, which is also the investment arm of the state council. These are, of course, only the tip of an iceberg. There are certainly tens of thousands of princelings, some of whom may have very "minor" pedigrees but who are nonetheless important in regional and local contexts.

Like other forms of inheritance, being a princeling is no guarantee of success in China's increasingly market driven business environment. According to Professor Li Cheng, a leading expert on China's leadership who teaches at Hamilton College, New York, being a princeling certainly means early advantages in terms of education opportunities and a "fast track" in career development. He points out, though, that to have lasting success as business executives, these princelings ultimately have to perform, just like anybody else.[7] This is just a fact of the market reality. Nonetheless, princelings' advantage of having better educational opportunities, high-level social networks and the ability to enjoy strong "connections" with the government where it counts means they enjoy better odds, everything else being equal, in performing well. In essence, this is the unique characteristic of how the inheritance pathway to affluence operates in China today.

Chart 3.1 illustrates the intricate pattern of how the three pathways to affluence, diverse as well as interconnected, have functioned in China since the 1980s.

Chart 3.1

China's Pathway to Affluent

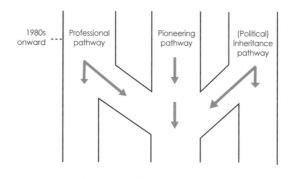

A PORTRAIT OF CHINA'S AFFLUENT CONSUMERS

Given how diverse the three pathways to affluence are, what are China's affluent consumers like? There is no shortage of stories of wealthy Chinese individuals, and their often extraordinary tales of how they have come to be where they are. From the point of view of market assessment, however, it is useful to have some general profiles that could guide businesses who target these affluent consumers as customers.

A portrait of China's affluent consumers can be gleaned from the results of a recent survey conducted in 10 cities that focused precisely on them.[8] The qualifying income level for survey respondents is $10,000 per year, which is higher than the $7,500 annual income threshold that is used to define the mass affluent. It is, however, close enough to generate a useful profile of China's affluent consumers.

To begin with, the respondents are strikingly young. Some 62% of them are between 25 and 34 years old. And another 23% are between 35 and 39 years old. In total, over 90% are below the age of 40. This finding is consistent with the "generational" perspective discussed above, which suggests that the younger generations, having better education and being more confident and ambitious, are better at taking advantage of new opportunities offered by the market economy in the past two decades.

Chart 3.2

China's Affluent Consumers

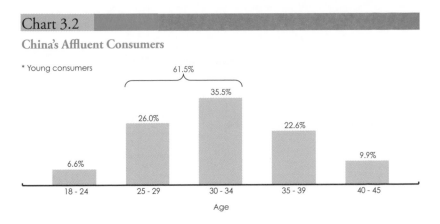

* Young consumers

The second striking feature is that they are extremely well educated. An impressive 65% of them have university and post-graduate levels of education. Only 7% are not high school graduates. This compares with an estimated 8% of the total population that are university educated, and some 15% with post-secondary education (but without university degrees).

Chart 3.3

China's Affluent Consumers

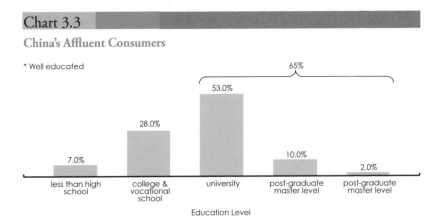

* Well educated

These affluent consumers are very media savvy. Internet usage is at 90% or above for all categories except one. Virtually all of them watch TV on a regular basis. Their readership of magazines is quite high, especially among those who are 18 to 24 and 30 to 45 years old. Their readership for newspapers, however, is quite low, dropping to 44% for those aged 25 to 29. For businesses keen to learn how to reach these affluent consumers, these patterns are worth watching.

Table 3.4
China's Affluent Consumers

* Media savvy

	Newspaper	Magazine	TV	Internet
18 - 24	84%	97%	98%	100%
25 - 29	44%	78%	97%	91%
30 - 34	64%	88%	98%	79%
35 - 39	94%	98%	99%	100%
40 - 45	77%	96%	100%	93%

In addition to being media savvy, they are also internet savvy. The vast majority, 71%, have email. About two-thirds use the internet to get news, while 63% use the internet to search for specific information.

Chart 3.5
China's Affluent Consumers

* Internet usage

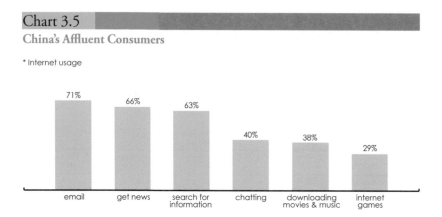

Apart from email and searching for information, 15% also engage in online shopping on a regular basis. Some 6% use the internet for job searching, maintaining a home page and for internet telephoney. Some 5% are involved in online education and training.

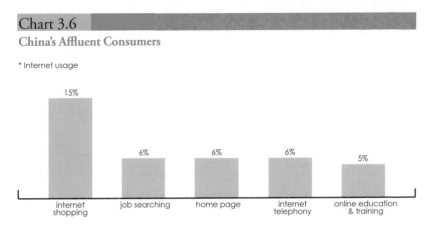

Chart 3.6
China's Affluent Consumers

* Internet usage

Dining out regularly appears to be very much a standard lifestyle for these affluent consumers. Dining out two to three times a week is a regular fare for 40%, while some 10%, amazingly, dine out more than five times a week. In other words, they rarely eat at home.

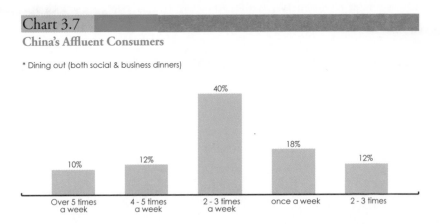

Chart 3.7
China's Affluent Consumers

* Dining out (both social & business dinners)

From the data collected the income thresholds for these affluent consumers to begin to adopt new consumption behavior can be estimated. It seems that they begin to acquire foreign currency accounts and international credit cards, and start to play golf when their annual income exceeds $21,000. At $22,000 annual income, they begin to travel overseas regularly. When their annual income exceeds $28,000, they begin to buy private condos, and at $30,000, imported cars. As it happens, most of them already own private cars. The survey data show that 81% of these affluent consumers own one private car, 8% two cars and 1% own more than two cars.

Chart 3.8
China's Affluent Consumers

* Annual income thresholds for adopting new consumption behavior

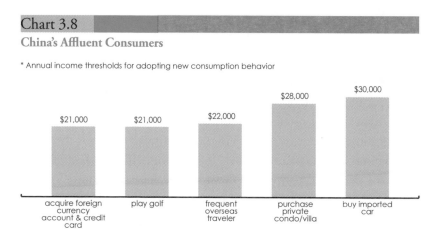

acquire foreign currency account & credit card	play golf	frequent overseas traveler	purchase private condo/villa	buy imported car
$21,000	$21,000	$22,000	$28,000	$30,000

Apart from being car owners, they are also property owners. More than half already own one property. An impressive 33% of them own two properties. And 10% own more than two properties. Only 5% of these affluent consumers do not own their own homes. This is a very high level of property ownership by any measure. What is more interesting, however, is their intention of buying more property in the next 12 months. Of those who currently own a single property, 21% reported that they plan to buy another property in the next 12 months. It is the same for those who currently own two properties. Among those who already own more than two properties, however, 34% reported that they plan to buy yet another property in the next 12 months. The pattern is, then, the more properties they own, the more they would like to buy.

Chart 3.9

China's Affluent Consumers

* Property ownership

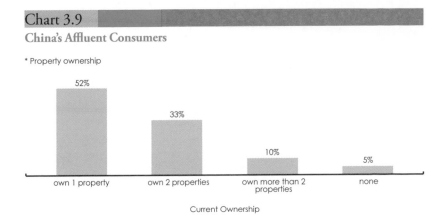

Current Ownership

As mentioned earlier, they become regular overseas travelers when their annual income exceeds $21,000. And it appears that as they become more seasoned as international travelers, their preferred destinations also expand. While Hong Kong still looms large as a preferred destination, new and more diverse locales such as Western Europe, Australia and Japan are now part of the mix. Interestingly, an exotic destination like the Maldives, a group of small islands in the midst of the Indian Ocean known for its fine beaches and diving sites, is among the top preferred destinations of China's affluent consumers.

Chart 3.10

China's Affluent Consumers

* Keen international travelers

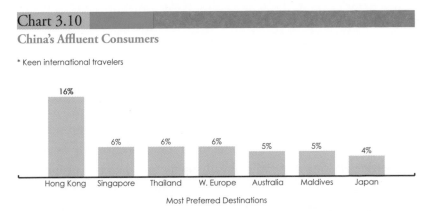

Most Preferred Destinations

And these affluent consumers are thoroughly digitalized. Practically all of them have a mobile phone, and 87% of them have laptop computers, while 73% have digital cameras. Digital video cameras, Bluetooth carphones and handheld devices are also popular.

Chart 3.11

China's Affluent Consumers

* Digital consumer electronics ownership

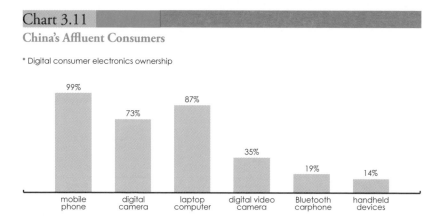

mobile phone	digital camera	laptop computer	digital video camera	Bluetooth carphone	handheld devices
99%	73%	87%	35%	19%	14%

While private insurance is still a relatively new financial product in China, it appears to have been well accepted by the affluent. Auto ownership clearly has been a strong catalyst-it made the purchase of auto insurance necessary. The purchase of injury insurance is also related to auto ownership. Life insurance, not directly associated with auto ownership, has been embraced by almost half of the affluent consumers. Over one-third of them have some forms of medical insurance, and 20% have property insurance.

Chart 3.12

China's Affluent Consumers

* Insurance purchase

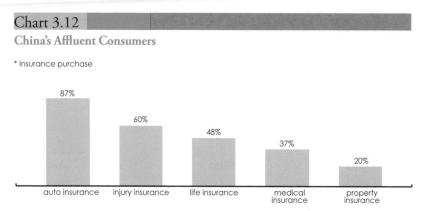

auto insurance	injury insurance	life insurance	medical insurance	property insurance
87%	60%	48%	37%	20%

Their investment portfolio remains relatively conservative, however. Over half of them have term deposits, a low yield and extremely risk-averse form of investment. Just under half own stocks, and only a quarter own mutual funds. Interestingly, while 22% own bonds, 18% reported real estate ownership as their form of investment. This overall conservatism could change quickly in the coming years when new investment products and wealth management services are introduced in China.

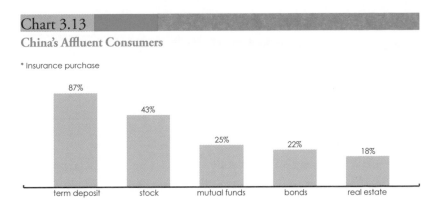

Chart 3.13

China's Affluent Consumers

* Insurance purchase

term deposit — 87%
stock — 43%
mutual funds — 25%
bonds — 22%
real estate — 18%

SIZE AND SPENDING POWER OF THE MASS AFFLUENT AND THE RICH

How big is the market of China's affluent consumers? The mass affluent, defined as those earning an annual income of between $7,500 and $50,000, was estimated at 12.8 million households in 2005, with a collective income of over $140 billion. Projecting forward with a trend rate of real GDP growth of 7.5% in the next 10 years, it is expected that there will be close to 50 million mass affluent households with an impressive collective income of over $500 billion.

Table 3.1

Size and Income of the Mass Affluent

Annual income $7,500 to $50,000 (2004 US$ & exchange rate)	2005	2015	Cumulative annual growth
Number of Households	12.6 million	44.9 million	13.6%
Total Household Income	$140.6 billion	$513.8 billion	13.8%
Average Annual Household Income	$11,120	$11,500	0.1%

(MasterCard Asia/Pacific)

The consumer market of the rich, defined as those earning an annual income of $50,000 and above, was estimated to have close to 48,000 households, with a collective income of almost $3 billion in 2005. Assuming the same trend rate of real GDP growth of 7.5% per year over the next 10 years, it is expected there will be over 400,000 such households in 2015, averaging an astonishing annual growth rate of 23.8%. Their collective income will also grow by about 10 times, exceeding $29 billion by 2015.

Table 3.2

Size and Income of the Rich

Annual income 50,000+ (constant 2004 US$)	2005	2015	Cumulative annual growth
Number of Households	47,900	405,200	23.8%
Total Household Income	$2.9 billion	$29.3 billion	26.0%
Average Annual Household Income	$59,700	$72,300	1.9%

(MasterCard Asia/Pacific)

At the apex of the rich households are a few hundred of China's richest families. The breakdown of the distribution of assets by industries of the 152 richest families in China is presented in Chart 3.14. Given China's rapid rate of urbanization, it is not surprising to find that 35% of the assets of these richest families are in real estate development. Manufacturing accounts for another 27%. IT, pharmaceuticals, media and tourism are all very low in their percentage share of assets. These may be, however, the new sunrise industries as China's economic growth increasingly broadens to the service sector. Hence, many new successful entrepreneurs will likely come from these industries in the coming years.

Chart 3.14
Size and Income of the Rich

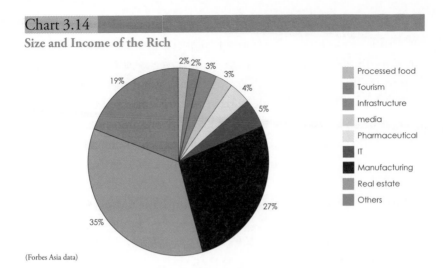

Legend:
- Processed food
- Tourism
- Infrastructure
- media
- Pharmaceutical
- IT
- Manufacturing
- Real estate
- Others

(Forbes Asia data)

Discretionary spending of the rich households, estimated at $18,900 per household in 2005, is projected to grow at double the rate of the mass affluent households, estimated at $3,600 in 2005. By 2015, the average discretionary spending per household will be $22,200 for the rich and only $3,500 for the mass affluent.

Table 3.3
Discretionary Spending Estimates

Per Household Discretionary Spending (constant 2004 US$)	2005	2015	Cumulative annual growth
The Mass Affluent	$3,600	$3,500	1.5%
The Rich	$18,900	$22,200	3.1%

(MasterCard Asia/Pacific)

About a quarter of the discretionary expenditure of the mass affluent is spent on automobiles, personal computers and mobile phones, and so on, making this their largest expenditure. This is followed by spending on travel and related leisure activities, with dining and entertaining close behind. Growth rates of all the discretionary expenditure items are expected to be similar, ranging between 13% and 14% per year for the next 10 years.

Table 3.4

Key Discretionary Expenditure of the Mass Affluent

Key discretionary Expenditure Items (2004 US$ billion)	2005	2015	Cumulative annual growth
Dining and entertaining	$9.7	$33.2	13.1%
Shopping	$5.9	$20.6	13.2%
Travel & Leisure	$10.4	$37.5	13.8%
Private Health & Luxury Medicine	$7.1	$25.8	14.0%
Automobiles, PCs & Mobile Phones, etc.	$11.3	$40.8	13.6%
Total	$44.4	$157.9	13.5%

(MasterCard Asia/Pacific)

In comparison, the rich households seem to have a more even spread in their discretionary spending; with the exception of shopping, spending on the top four key expenditure items is estimated to be about equal. All five items, however, will enjoy very high rates of growth at around 25.5% to 26% per year in the coming decade. By 2015, some $9 billion will be spent by these 400,000 households on five key discretionary expenditure items.

Table 3.5

Key Discretionary Expenditure of the Rich

Key discretionary Expenditure Items (2004 US$ billion)	2005	2015	Cumulative annual growth
Dining and Entertaining	$0.2	$1.9	25.4%
Shopping	$0.1	$1.2	25.5%
Travel & Leisure	$0.2	$2.1	26.0%
Private Health & Luxury Medicine	$0.2	$1.5	26.1%
Automobiles, PCs & Mobile Phones, etc.	$0.2	$2.3	26.0%
Total	$0.9	$9.0	25.8%

(MasterCard Asia/Pacific)

In spite of their diverse backgrounds and generational differences, the mass affluent and the rich consumers of China share one thing in common. Due to their shared history of half a century of socialist suppression of private wealth and enterprise, in a fundamental sense they are all *nouveau riche*, and being rich for the first time, and they can't wait to tell everyone about it. Chinese consumers therefore have a single minded focus on designer branded products—because these are seen as providing instant proof of their status of new wealth and success. Thus, in many ways and among the mass affluent more so than among the rich, the louder the product screams "I am expensive" the stronger its appeal.

In indulging themselves with their new wealth, successful first generation entrepreneurs in China often have unusual tastes, and they are not shy in showing off. For example, the successful Beijing construction businessman mentioned above, Liu Zhifang, fancies horse breeding. As a boy growing up in a village outside of Beijing, he was around horses and rode them regularly. While his nostalgia led him back to horses, his wealth has set his sights higher. Instead of the everyday ponies that he rode, he now breeds racehorses. In 2002, he invested $1.25 million to set up a stud farm and racing center to breed what he hopes to be the best racehorses of China. He believes that he is a pioneer in creating a horse culture and industry in China and is proud of that fact.

China's affluent consumer market will certainly evolve quickly, like everything else, over the next decade. It is reasonable to expect that the crass *nouveau riche* attitude so prevalent today will be increasingly tempered by sophistication and more nuanced tastes and styles; and more likely to be so among the half-million-strong rich households. Accordingly, businesses catering to these customers must stay abreast of the changes in order to be relevant and successful in this exciting, dynamic and rapidly expanding consumer market.

INDIA'S AFFLUENT CONSUMERS 4

One fine spring morning in 1981, a group of business executives was granted a rare audience with the then-prime minister of India, Mrs. Indira Gandhi. The audience took place in the lush sprawling garden of the prime minister's residence in Delhi, lined with dazzling marigolds. Gandhi wore an elegant white Bengal cotton sari, looking at once relaxed and regal. In over two decades of involvement in India's political life, Gandhi had proved to be a remarkably shrewd and masterful politician, capable of being bold and decisive; but unfortunately, she was also capable of colossal mistakes in judgments.

She had just been swept back into power in the 1980 election, cloaking herself with the mantle of the champion of the poor, and she was enjoying a new wave of popularity. As the daughter of Nehru, the founding prime minister of India, she learned the craft of political power early. After her mother died when she was just 18, she became her father's confidante, travel companion and personal assistant. Taking over the leadership of the Congress Party shortly after Nehru's death, she soon became prime minister, thus continuing the Nehru political dynasty.

She led India in a short but vicious war with Pakistan in 1970, which resulted in the dismemberment of Pakistan and the creation of Bangladesh, earning her great prestige. Her reputation was further enhanced by India's successful explosion of a nuclear device in 1974. Playing the Cold War card, she showed defiance to the US, which did her no harm among those harboring anti-American sentiments.

But she became increasingly autocratic, concentrating ever more power in her own hands. Enraged by a court ruling that she had committed some minor voting irregularities in her home district in 1975, she declared a state of emergency, suspended civil liberties and introduced censorship, and ruled as a virtual dictator. Mounting public outcry forced her to relent and call a new election in 1977 in which she was decisively defeated. But the coalition that replaced her soon fell apart. Gandhi, ever resourceful, won the election in 1980 and returned to power feeling fully vindicated.

Meeting the group of business executives on this fine spring morning was more a public relations exercise than anything else. Gandhi was not interested in seeking advice from them on how to run the economy. She was keen on continuing her father's program of economic planning and pervasive government regulations. As recounted by Gurcharan Das,[1] the audience started with several sycophants singing Gandhi's praises, lauding her various achievements. Then there was an embarrassing silence. Finally, a few executives spoke up, Das himself included, in delicately diplomatic terms, questioning the government's management of the economy. They questioned in particular the stifling effect of the licensing system, under which practically every business operation, from starting a new company to introducing a new product by an existing company, required a government license. These licenses were rationed by the bureaucracy, which turned bureaucrats into powerful czars who had more power than the owners and executives in running their businesses. They also questioned India's restrictive control over foreign investment and ownership, and why the tax burdens had to be so heavy for businesses.

Gandhi deftly deflected the questions, making no concession to the slightest possibility that the government might have made any mistake. She eloquently argued that licenses were important, otherwise unscrupulous businessmen, driven by greed, would over-invest and create overcapacity. That would be wasteful. Foreign encroachment into the Indian economy should be limited; it was fine for foreign companies to bring new technologies to India, but for them to make huge profits from exploiting India's poor and take market shares away from Indian companies was not to be tolerated. Taxing businesses was merely to ensure that they contributed their proper share to the building and running of India. Lowering business tax would simply raise business profit margins; no one else would benefit.

There is no reason to doubt that Gandhi sincerely believed in her pat answers to the executives' questions. If nothing else, she was a good keeper of her father's economic legacy. Years before, Nehru had written to a young and impressionable Indira in a letter that if businesses were left to operate freely without government supervision and planning, the result would be the squandering of India's meager resources.

When independence came in 1947, it was abundantly clear to the new Indian government, led by Nehru, that poverty was the single most daunting problem facing the new nation. To

Nehru, the answer was also clear-comprehensive planning and state-led industrialization. Never sympathetic to businessmen and the private sector, Nehru had come under the influence of British Fabian socialism from an early age (ironically some of the strongest allies and supporters of Mahatma Gandhi's independence struggle had been leading Indian businessmen). Impressed by the Soviet Union, he readily adopted central planning and five-year plans. He wanted a "scientific" solution to India's problem of mass poverty and backwardness.

And Nehru had exactly the scientist he needed for his ambitious "scientific" program to eradicate poverty in India. P.C. Mahalanobis was a brilliant Cambridge-trained physicist. Appointed by Nehru to direct India's central planning, he masterminded the creation of India's highly quantitative planning models, with complicated and intricate input-output matrices and mathematical equations; he treated the economy with the precision of running an experiment in physics. The epicenter of all these efforts was the Planning Commission, established in 1950 and chaired by Nehru himself, which became the real manager of the economy. A huge planning bureaucracy grew in the ensuing years.

In the first two decades after Independence, planning begat planning, and the state got more and more involved in the detail operations of the economy. Famous titles of government reports during this period told the story: *The Mahalanobis Committee*, 1964; *The Monopolies Inquiry Commission*, 1965; *The Hazari Committee*, 1966; *The Dutt Committee on Licensing*, 1969. All are elaborate plans, recommendations, and justifications for more government regulations and control of the economy.

Even as the role of the state in the economy was expanding inexorably, signs of failure were everywhere. Central planning and a bloated bureaucracy saddled India with an enormously complex and cumbersome system that businesses and citizens had to deal with on a day-to-day basis. Regulations, quotas, permits, tariffs and licenses proliferated in a Byzantine maze, often in intertwined fashion. Frequently a license could only be granted if a quota had already been secured. Securing the quota, however, required that official approval be already in place ascertaining that certain regulations had been met. To ascertain meeting the regulations in turn required... and so on. Getting the runaround was not just a metaphor, but a literal truth.

An immediate victim was India's entrepreneurial energy. Entrepreneurial initiatives were being sapped; and, even more damagingly, distorted. Enterprising entrepreneurs competed for government favors and for the all-important licenses and permits, instead of competing in the market place. Honest entrepreneurs spent their valuable time and resources preparing and submitting proposals to government agencies and bureaucrats; dishonest ones resorted to bribes and other unsavory means to get ahead of competitors. Tata Sons, a leading business house in India and universally respected for their integrity and good corporate citizenship, reportedly submitted 119 proposals between 1960 and 1989 to start new businesses or to expand existing ones. Undoubtedly all these proposals were submitted in strictly professional manner completely untainted by any hint of corruption. All were rejected.[2] One can only wonder how many new jobs and how much income would have been created in India had a fraction of these proposals been approved.

It is ironic that while Nehru's original vision of comprehensive planning was meant to facilitate the applications of science and technology to drive India's economic development and fast-track its social progress, the actual result was technological retardation. An enduring symbol of this perverse outcome was the domestically manufactured car "Ambassador," modeled on the British Austin of the late 1950s. It was virtually the only sedan car model that was allowed to be produced in India for three decades, and became ubiquitous on India's streets. It retained the same design for all those years, when auto technology outside of India went through several generations of revolutionary changes. To add insult to injury, Indian car buyers had to wait long periods, sometimes years, for delivery of such a technologically obsolete, fuel inefficient, inferior and uncomfortable vehicle.

Instead of dynamic changes envisioned by Nehru's comprehensive planning, stagnation became the norm. India's snail pace of growth, hovering around 3% a year, had become known embarrassingly as the "Hindu rate of growth." Nehru's dislike of competition emasculated India's entrepreneurial energy and subverted it into underhanded dealings in briberies and collusions between businesses and bureaucrats in a whole host of corrupt practices. He and advisors like P.C. Mahalanobis had also misjudged the potential of exports and how it could energize the Indian economy and deliver higher growth. When the East Asian tigers surged ahead, India stagnated. By the early 1980s, tiny Hong Kong with a then-population of some six million, was exporting more to the global market than the whole of India. By the late 1980s, many Indians, including some of the country's most visionary industrialists as well as the best educated young professionals, had given up on India. Indian businessmen sought opportunities outside of India, and young Indian professionals sought employment overseas.

Extensive state ownership in industries meant inefficiency and poor quality products, and frequently no product at all. The height of absurdity was probably the state-owned Hindustan Fertilizer Corporation. It was built by the government between 1971 and 1979 with machinery imported from Germany, Czechoslovakia and Poland, with considerable public funds. It employed 1,200 workers, and they had been dutifully reporting for work ever since the factory opened in 1980. In every aspect it appeared to be a normal sort of state-run industrial plant, except for one anomaly: it had never produced a single grain of fertilizer. It turned out that the machinery imported by the government bureaucrats could not be made to fit together, so the plant never managed to function.[3] However, it was government-owned, and therefore the workers must be paid; and its theoretical output made for a nice statistical addition to the government's planned expansion of industrial capacity as part of the five-year plan. Everyone was happy—the workers who were paid for doing nothing, the politicians who "created" the jobs, and the bureaucrats who somehow "met" the plan for industrial expansion— and the Indian economy suffered.

Gandhi was assassinated in 1984, killed by her own Sikh bodyguards in revenge for her order to attack the Golden Temple in Amritsar, (the Sikhs' sacred shrine), to root out Sikh militants. Her son and Prime Minister Rajiv Gandhi was assassinated in 1991, killed by a suicide bomber from the Tamil Tigers, in revenge for his decision to send the army to Sri Lanka to try to stop its civil war. These two assassinations truncated the Nehru dynasty's grip on Indian politics. A Congress Party stalwart, P.V. Narasimha Rao, already in his 70s, became the prime minister. He was widely expected not to last long, perhaps just there to warm the seat until one of the younger Nehrus was ready to get back into the driver's seat to continue the family dynasty. In fact, Rao was plucked from near retirement to lead the government after Rajiv's assassination precisely because he was seen as a loyal functionary, a conciliator and unlikely to challenge the status quo. Instead, Rao served the full five-year term while fundamentally redirecting the Indian economy away from government planning and control to market liberalization and reform.

A crisis presented the opportunity for bold actions. The making of the crisis had started before Rao became prime minister. On

August 2, 1990, Saddam Hussein ordered the Iraqi army to invade Kuwait. The price of oil spiked and hit India's balance of payment hard. It was further compounded by a precipitous drop of remittance payments by Indian workers in the Middle East. By the time Rao was sworn in as prime minister, India's foreign reserve was down to the equivalent of two weeks' imports. The country was on the verge of bankruptcy. Rao needed someone to take charge to stop the Indian economy from falling off the cliff. And he needed him fast.

It was under such inauspicious circumstances that Manmohan Singh became finance minister. Born in a poor part of rural Punjab, Singh made his way in the world from his humble beginning armed with only talent and effort. A brilliant student, he won a scholarship to study at Cambridge, and after graduating with a degree in economics, he went on to earn his Ph.D. at Oxford. Returning to India, he enjoyed a successful career as an economic bureaucrat, rising through the ranks to hold a senior post at the Planning Commission. Soft-spoken and ever-diplomatic, Singh was known for both his brilliance in economics and a non-confrontational style. Yet, he rose to the occasion when appointed finance minister, and acted with uncharacteristic speed. And so it happened that Rao and Singh and a small core of like-minded officials became the unlikely, and sometimes reluctant, champions of economic reform.

In presenting his emergency budget in July 1991, Singh minced no words to point out that the country was a mess and in danger of economic implosion, and reform was the only hope. He was shrewd enough to invoke the names of Nehru, Gandhi and Rajiv Gandhi to bless the reform, as if his radical agenda had always been meant by them. In spite of the meager support that Rao had within the Congress Party and the skepticism of many of the Congress old guards, Rao and Singh managed to secure parliamentary approval of the reform program, made easier by the crisis atmosphere.

Within weeks, the Rao government devalued the rupee, cut subsidies, reduced tariffs, and, most importantly, eliminated licenses for about 80% of industry. In one stroke, it freed Indian industry from the stranglehold of the "license raj." Now companies could expand and diversify in response to market conditions without having to first secure licenses for doing so. The reformers even dared to go as far as to relax restriction on foreign investment, however tentatively, and to signal the beginning of divesting government's shares in companies. As subsequent events showed, the impact on India's economy was profound.

In spite of widespread state ownership in the economy, one thing that Nehru never did was to nationalize private industries (the few exceptions include the nationalization of Tata's Air India). As a consequence a group of large industrial conglomerates, led by legendary entrepreneurial dynasties like the Tatas and the Birlas, built by their illustrious founding patriarchs during colonial times, retained their assets and continued to operate within the framework of Nehru's comprehensive planning and the license raj, albeit in severely limited ways. The reform of 1991 immediately benefited these industrial conglomerates, freeing them to expand and to go into new businesses.

One new industry also benefited-the embryonic information technology (IT) industry. India's IT businesses had a relatively easier time under the license raj simply because it was so new that it was not listed among the industries to be directly regulated. It did not mean, however, that it was easy to run an IT business under the license raj. For example, in the 1980s Narayana Murthy, the legendary founder of Infosys, one of India's leading IT companies and the first Indian firm to list on the US stock market, had to make 50 trips over a period of two years traveling from Bangalore, where Infosys is based, to Delhi to meet with central government bureaucrats in order to get a permit to import a computer worth $1,500. The 1991 reform immediately eased import restrictions and lowered communications costs, which dramatically improved the operational environment of the IT industry. The devaluation of the rupee in turn made India's IT service exports even more competitive globally. The result was an extraordinary and explosive growth of India's IT industry, propelling it within the decade to becoming a world leader.

Ironically it was Nehru who laid the groundwork for the emergence of this archetypal modern Indian industry. As part of his drive of using science and technology to eradicate poverty, Nehru set up the Indian Institute of Technology (IIT) in 1952, modeled after the Massachusetts Institute of Technology (MIT). In subsequent decades, IIT grew to become a premier training ground for India's brightest students in science and engineering, especially in computer science and related disciplines. IIT started to supply the nascent domestic IT firms with superb human resources. This supply of cheap and world-class brain power caught the attention of multinational firms. The arrival in Bangalore of Texas Instruments in 1985, the first IT multinational to invest in India, put Bangalore on the map and signaled India's rise as a global IT power. The 1991 reform accelerated the process that had already been underway for some years. Soon Bangalore became known as India's Silicon Valley.

The decade and a half in India since the 1991 reform has been nothing if not tumultuous. On the political front, Rao's Congress-led government was replaced by the BJP government, which, to the surprise of many, continued with the reform agenda set by Rao's government. When the BJP government campaigned to be re-elected, they were proudly proclaiming "India shining." Then they fell, defeated by disgruntled voters, especially those in rural areas, whose India was actually not at all shining. A rejuvenated Congress Party chose Sonja Gandhi, Rajiv's Italy-born widow, to be its leader, and formed the next government in partnership with a group of leftist parties, including the communist party. For a few drama-filled weeks, it looked as if India would have an Italian woman as prime minister. Then Sonja Gandhi decided to stay as the leader of the Congress Party, and Manmohan Singh, finance minister under Rao and one of the key architects of the 1991 reform, became the new prime minister in 2004.

On the ground, the Indian economy had been unquestionably transformed. Growth rates shot up to reach 6% real GDP growth per year, and more recently, to 8%-plus . Exports, led by the highly successful IT sector, rose to exceed $40 billion a year. Foreign direct investment, started from virtually zero, grew to about $5 billion a year in the past few years. Dynamic changes are clearly visible in urban centers like Delhi, Mumbai, Bangalore and Chennai. While it is true that a great deal more has to be done in furthering reform, particularly in improving public infrastructure, reducing labor market rigidity, and remedying grave deficiencies in general education-the fact is that for the younger and better educated Indians in urban areas, opportunities have never been better. These changes, while raising income for a significant portion of Indians in general, have also eased the way for an increasing number of them to join the rank of the mass affluent. How the three pathways to affluence operate today in India has been profoundly changed.

THE INHERITANCE PATHWAY TO AFFLUENCE

If there is a business aristocracy in India, it would have to be the Tatas. The Tata business dynasty was founded in 1868 by Jamsetji Tata, thus making the business 138 years old in 2006. The Tatas are Parsees of Persian descent, whose ancestors fled Persia after the Muslim conquest, keen to preserve their traditional Zoroastrian religion instead of converting to Islam. The refugees, when they arrived in the west coast of India, were granted refuge by the local maharaja to settle in Gujarat. They were called Parsees after the province of Pars in Persia where they came from.

Jamsetji started in textiles, then quickly expanded into trading, establishing a stronghold in Bombay (Mumbai today). From the beginning, the Tatas ran their business with a strong sense of social welfare for their workers. Jamsetji introduced pensions for workers in his textile mills in 1886, and accident compensation in 1895, way ahead of his times, and certainly ahead of any other Indian business houses.[4] This tradition has abided through vastly changed economic and political times and business conditions in the past 138 years, even as the business, Tata Sons, has grown to become one of India's leading business houses, with activities spanning heavy industry, manufacturing, chemicals, agribusiness, financial services, hospitality and IT.

As a business house Tata Sons has been famous for its entrepreneurial energy and vision. Again, Jamsetji set the pattern. After being refused entry to a hotel reserved for the British in Bombay, he built the legendary Taj Mahal Hotel on the waterfront of the bustling city, opposite the India Gate. The Taj chain of hotels and resorts today is among the best in India and neighboring countries. J.R.D. Tata, two generations and a few decades later, pioneered commercial aviation in India, winning the colonial government's grudging approval (but nationalized by Nehru after independence). Tata Sons is also a leader in India's IT sector today.

Ratan Tata, the current chairman of Tata Sons, took the reins in the 1980s and started a remarkable process of rejuvenating the moribund business that seemed to have lost focus and been suffocating under the license raj. Educated at Cornell University and Harvard Business School, Ratan Tata began to professionalize management, and moved to invest aggressively and successfully in the booming IT sector by launching Tata Consulting, which has since become a global leader in IT software and services. Seizing opportunities opened up by reform in the 1990s, Tata Sons expanded into financial services to take advantage of rising domestic purchasing power, and is also planning a "people's car" that could be sold for $2,000 each. Equally active overseas, Tata Consulting is a leading investor in China in the IT sector; and an ambitious multibillion-dollar plan to invest in neighboring Bangladesh was unveiled in 2005.

A key beneficiary of the financial success of a rejuvenated Tata Sons are the two Tata Trusts, which hold 63% of the shares of Tata Sons, and are wholly devoted to philanthropic work, consistent with the Tata tradition of caring for the masses. This is unique among all Indian business houses. Other beneficiaries are, of course, shareholders of Tata Sons, the biggest being the Mistry family, which holds some 18% of the shares. It is, however, in the expansion of a professionalized management and better paid employment created in technical areas that Tata Sons is opening up the professional pathway to affluence for tens and thousands of well-educated and skilled workers. Hence, as the Tatas and their large shareholders continue to travel on the inheritance pathway to affluence, they are also opening up the professional pathway to affluence for a whole new generation of Indians.

Another venerable name in Indian business is the Birlas, founded by G.D. Birla in Calcutta in 1923. The family fortune was founded in textiles and fertilizers. Operating under the restrictive hand of the license raj in the 1960s, the Birlas felt they had to expand outside of India. Under the guidance of the MIT-educated Aditya, a third-generation Birla, the business ventured first to Thailand, then Malaysia, Indonesia and the Philippines; expanding into palm oil, cement and mining. Over a period of 25 working years, Aditya Birla achieved the enviable record of having built 70 industrial plants; unfortunately for the Indian economy, many were located overseas. At the time of his early death in 1995, he was moving into oil refining, copper smelting and steel. Kumar Mangalam Birla, then age 27 and a fourth-generation Birla, took over. Under his leadership the business both expanded and consolidated, and the management has also been professionalized. In 1999, the Birla Management Center was created to make key decisions for the group, and Kumar Birla brought in the former Hindustan Lever director Debu Bhattacharya as managing director.[5]

An immediate effect of the 1990s reform has been the rejuvenation of India's traditional business dynasties like the Tatas and the Birlas. As their examples show, they have taken advantage of new opportunities opened up by reform to expand while professionalizing their management. In so doing, they are creating the conditions for the professional pathway to affluence to become available to tens and thousands of new entrants who gain a chance to be one of the mass affluent, something that was undreamt of before.

THE PIONEERING PATHWAY TO AFFLUENCE

In 1981, Narayana Murthy and six partners set up Infosys in a garage in the southern India city of Pune with $1,500. The seed capital came from their private savings since no banks would consider extending them a business loan. A graduate of the Indian Institute of Management (IIM), Murthy led Infosys to grow from strength to strength, even though he had to frequently suffer the indignity of having to deal with Delhi bureaucrats. Infosys is now a household name and a company listed on the New York Stock Exchange with annual revenues of billions of dollars; and it counts the world's leading companies as its clients for whom Infosys develops proprietary software. In 2006, Murthy stepped down from directly running the company to be its "chief mentor," a concept more Californian than Indian.

Murthy is one of the many brilliant Indian entrepreneurs who successfully rode the new wave of information technology and the internet to establish world-class businesses, amass fabulous personal fortunes, and create hundreds of thousands of well paid jobs for young and well trained Indians. Other legendary names include Shiv Nadar, the founder of HCL, India's leading computer company; Azim Premji, the founder of Wirpo; and the Raju family who founded Satyam Computers, to name just a few.

This wave of entrepreneurship was made possible because of a convergence of three factors. The first is India's technical brain power, nurtured by elite institutions like IIT, which formed an unbeatable competitive advantage when combined with the rock-bottom wages of India.[6] The second is the fortuitous fact that the comprehensive planning and the license raj had not anticipated the emergence of the IT industry. Although they also had to struggle with red tape and bureaucratic inertia, IT entrepreneurs were able to operate with relative ease. The third factor is the timely emergence of the internet, which became the virtual highway for India's IT exports. The 1990s reform merely accelerated what was by then a rapidly expanding new industry in India. Within a decade, IT service exports grew from virtually nothing to more than $40 billion a year. The types of service export have also been evolving-moving from basic services like call centers to increasingly sophisticated, and higher value-added, business process outsourcing. Centers like Bangalore and Chennai have become booming hubs of a dynamic industry. The IT industry, while building huge personal fortunes for the successful pioneers, has also become the standard path to mass affluence for young and well educated Indians.

There has been, however, a completely different way to succeed as pioneering entrepreneurs under the license raj as exemplified by the rise of Dhirubhai Ambani. Born to a humble school teacher in a village in Gujarat, as a young man Dhirubhai worked for eight years in Aden in the Middle East in a variety of menial jobs for Arab merchants and traders in oil and textiles. Returning to India in the 1960s, he set himself up as a trader in the then Bombay, touting his

Middle East connections as an asset. What set him apart from the crowd of all the other traders, everyone as sharp and shrewd as the next, was that he was able to find a way to work the license raj to his advantage-amassing a personal fortune and making a mockery of Nehru's comprehensive planning.

Operating out of a borrowed pigeon-hole of an "office" in Bombay's Bhaat Bazaar, he spent the day chewing paan and drinking tea with other bazaar traders, scheming deals that would allow him to bypass government regulations or subverting them to his own advantage. The opportunity came with the new synthetic yarn. Dhirubhai was convinced that synthetic yarn would take off in India with its bright colors, durability and wrinkle-free quality. India's urban middle class would love it. And he had already accumulated some $7,500 of savings from his trading profits. He was ready to take the plunge.

He invested in a small but technologically advanced textile mill near Ahmedabad, and immediately ran into problems with licenses. Manufacturing synthetic yarn required imports of synthetic fiber and related raw materials. All such imports were tightly controlled by quotas and licenses. It was common for many Indian firms to resort to smuggling when faced with shortages. Exporters were, however, issued with "replenishment licenses," called REPs, allowing them to import with a portion of their export earnings. These REPs were not meant to be transferred. But Dhirubhai found a way to buy up REPs from other exporters (and many of his critics accused him of using bribes and other unsavory means to do so), and very soon he was in control of the supply of synthetic fibers in India, which allowed him to both run his mill and make huge profits.

Dhirubhai then started moving upstream. Working hand-in-glove with senior government officials in Gandhi's government,

Dhirubhai received the unusual permission to build and operate a plant to produce synthetic fiber; which in turn authorized him to import another set of closely controlled raw materials, including the polyester filament yarn that was in chronic short supply in India, with a domestic price six times higher than the world price. He then effectively became the monopoly supplier of polyester filament fiber and it really made his fortune. This set the pattern of how he operated in the environment of the license raj: moving upstream in production, from textiles to polyesters, to chemicals, to petroleum; and each step of the way he always managed to acquire the needed licenses to operate, often putting him in the position of monopoly supplier in the tightly regulated Indian economy. And he ruthlessly exploited again and again his monopoly position to earn huge profits.

He took his company, Reliance, public in 1977, and paid high dividends and bonus issues to keep his 2.6 million shareholders happy. As a publicity stunt he once rented an entire sport stadium to hold Reliance's annual general meeting, to the delight of his many shareholders. In spite of being dubbed by some Indian media as being the head of an "evil empire" that ran on bribes and corrupt practices, Dhirubhai remained a popular corporate hero to his shareholders and admirers.

Dhirubhai died in 2002 and set off a public feud between his two sons, Anil and Mukesh. It resulted in the breakup of the business into two, with Mukesh Ambani in control of the larger share, the Reliance Industries (mostly in petrochemicals). It is now India's largest private sector enterprise with $20 billion of revenue in 2005, accounting for some 3.5% of India's GDP. Now Mukesh Ambani is developing a grandiose plan to integrate India's farm and retail sector with an ambitious program of infrastructure building. If successful, it would help transform India's backward agricultural sector.[7]

While making the fortunes for entrepreneurs like Dhirubhai Ambani, India's license raj also drove some of India's best pioneering entrepreneurs out of the country. The extraordinary story of the Mittal steel fortune is a case in point. Mohan Lal Mittal founded Ispat Group to make steel in the 1950s. Mittal, a member of the Marwari ethnic group, famous for their clan-based business connections,[8] started out in Rajasthan, and then moved to set up his base in Bombay. His son, Lakshmi, joined the family business in 1970. At about the same time, father and son had come to the conclusion that they could not expand in India due to onerous government regulations, and they must therefore go overseas. They invested in Indonesia in the early 1970s and it proved to be successful. They then built steel plants in Trinidad and Tobago; followed by buying facilities in Mexico and Canada, with Lakshmi Mittal driving the international side of the family business.

In the early 1990s, Lakshmi moved into Europe, taking over first Hamburger Stahlwere in Germany and Irish Steel in Ireland. He moved to be based in London in 1996, and listed Ispat International in 1997, raising $776 million with a 20% IPO. His rapid expansion was accomplished with bold and visionary acquisitions. A case in point is the purchase of the Karmet plant in Kazakhstan in 1995. Kazakhstan was literally a frontier territory for international investment at the time, having just become independent following the breakup of the USSR. Mittal took advantage of a Kazakhstan government keen for foreign investment and the fact that practically no other international business was there, and acquired a six-million-ton capacity plant on very favorable terms.

Mittal joined the top league of international steel makers when he took over Inland Steel in 1998 for $14 billion, the sixth largest steel producer in the US with an annual capacity of five million tons. He quickly consolidated his US production with those in Mexico,

Canada and the Caribbean, gaining stronger pricing power and economies of scale. Now he was ready to aim to become the world's number one steel producer. Success came in 2006 when he bid for the Luxembourg-based Arcelor, Europe's largest steel producer. After an acrimonious boardroom battle, Mittal Steel, which was 90% owned by Lakshmi Mittal, merged with Arcelor to create Arcelor Mittal, with Lakshmi owning 45% of the new company.[9]

It is ironic that India's license raj, by driving the Mittals overseas, indirectly helped to create an international business powerhouse that probably would not have happened had they stayed in India. The fact is that the Mittals are not alone. The size of the Indian business diaspora has been estimated to number as high as 20 million people, with a combined gross asset of $300 billion in the late 1990s.[10] The hope today is that with reform, they will return to India with investment and international business contacts in increasing numbers, thereby creating a more dynamic environment for other aspiring Indians to succeed.

THE PROFESSIONAL PATHWAY TO AFFLUENCE

The main roads in Bangalore are lined with sparkling new steel and glass head offices of IBM, Oracle, SAP and a host of leading international IT companies, alongside campuses of Indian IT giants like Infosys and Wirpo. Tens of thousands of well paid new technical and managerial jobs are being created each year by these companies. They are the points of entry for well educated and skilled Indians to join the ranks of the mass affluent, defined as households earning between $7,500 and $50,000 per year.[11]

On the supply side it is estimated that each year there are some 440,000 university graduates with degrees in technical disciplines such as computer sciences and engineering; 300,000 receiving their post graduate degrees, and about 2.3 million of university graduates with non-technical degrees.[12] They add up to over three million graduates a year. It is a well known fact that the quality of graduates vary widely between world class institutions like IIT and IIM, and business operators issuing bogus degrees. So assuming conservatively that only a quarter of the graduates are of high standards, it nevertheless translates into 760,000 graduates per year.

On the demand side, booming business means chronic shortages of adequate human resources to staff the rapidly expanding operations, in spite of the apparently large number of high quality graduates per year. Staff attrition rates have been reported to be as high as 60% in some of the firms that supply business process outsourcing services. This means only one thing, rising wages. For the well trained and qualified, the professional pathway to affluence is literally operating in full throttle today.

Chart 4.1 illustrates how the three pathways to affluence are working in mutually reinforcing ways to swell the ranks of the mass affluent and the rich. Prior to the beginning of reform, the inheritance pathway was the way to be rich for the exclusive few. Equally exclusive were the pioneering entrepreneurs who could work the license raj to their advantage. Under such conditions, while a few could get fabulously rich, mass affluence was not possible. Things started to change when IT entrepreneurs began to grow in numbers and expand the size of their businesses, and the traditional business houses became rejuvenated with reform. Demand for technical professionals and managers grew rapidly, thus opening up the professional pathway to affluence. Some of those succeeding through the professional pathway then turned pioneering entrepreneurs, taking their chances in starting up their own businesses, thus adding momentum to the pioneering pathway to affluence.

Chart 4.1

India's Path to Affluence

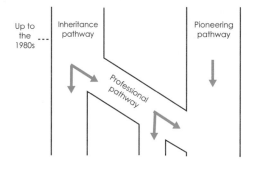

MARKET SIZE OF THE MASS AFFLUENT AND RICH HOUSEHOLDS

How big is the size of the mass affluent today? Using the annual household income bracket of $7,500 to $50,000 as definition, it is estimated that there were 5.2 million mass affluent households in India in 2005, accounting for 2.7% of total households. Their number is projected to grow to 10.5 million in 2015, accounting for 4.6% of total households. The average income of these households is estimated to have been $11,554 in 2005, and rising to $11,912 in 2015.

Table 4.1

Size and Income of the Mass Affluent

Annual income $7,500 to $50,000 (2004 US$ & exchange rate)	2005	2015	Average annual growth
Number of Households	5.2 million	10.5 million	7.3%
Total Household Income	$59.1 billion	$124.6 billion	7.7%
Average Annual Household Income	$11,554	$11,912	0.3%

(MasterCard Asia/Pacific)

The rich households, defined as those with annual income of more than $50,000, numbered 145,000 in 2005, and are expected to increase to 405,000 in 2015. They account for only a very small percentage of total households, however. In 2005, they accounted for 0.08% of total households, and in 2015 they are expected to account for 0.18% of total households. Their average household income, however, is significant at around $63,000 in 2005, and is expected to be about the same in real terms in 2015. Collectively, however, their income is massive—$9.4 billion in 2005 and almost $26 billion in 2015.

Table 4.2

Size and Income of the Rich

Annual income $50,000+ (constant 2004 US$)	2005	2015	Average annual growth
Number of Households	145,000	405,500	8.3%
Total Household Income	$9.4 billion	$25.9 billion	10.7%
Average Annual Household Income	$63,180	$63,975	0.1%

(MasterCard Asia/Pacific)

At the apex of these rich households are the 40 richest, ranked by Forbes on an annual basis. Many of them are in the billionaire category, while the "poorest" of them are worth a few hundred million dollars each. The breakdown of their industries is shown in Chart 4.2. It is significant to note that some 17% of the 40 richest in India in 2005 made their fortunes in IT, even though it is such a new industry. This illustrates the power of how the pioneering pathway to affluence has been operating in the recent past.

Chart 4.2

Industry Sectors of the richest families in India (2005)

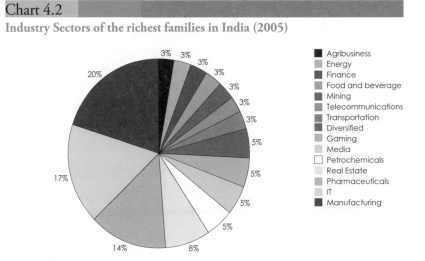

Agribusiness
Energy
Finance
Food and beverage
Mining
Telecommunications
Transportation
Diversified
Gaming
Media
Petrochemicals
Real Estate
Pharmaceuticals
IT
Manufacturing

(*Forbes Asia*, "Top 40 richest in 2005")

The estimated discretionary spending per household for the mass affluent was quite impressive at $3,700 in 2005, and is expected to rise to almost $5,000 in 2015. Similarly, the average discretionary spending of the rich households is estimated at $21,400 and $27,000 respectively, in 2005 and 2015. It should be noted that the average is very deceptive in this case as the definition of the "rich" starts with an annual income of $50,000, and goes to as high as several hundreds of million dollars at the top, such as among the 40 richest families. One can only imagine the amount of discretionary spending power held by the top rich families.

Table 4.3

Discretionary Spending Estimates

Per Household Discretionary Spending (constant 2004 US$)	2005	2015	Average annual growth
The Mass Affluent	$3,700	$4,900	2.8%
The Rich	$21,400	$27,000	2.3%

(MasterCard Asia/Pacific)

For the mass affluent, their spending on key discretionary expenditure items is shown in Table 4.4. While dining and entertainment and shopping are the top expenditure items, it is travel and leisure activities, at a compound annual growth rate of 15.2%, that will grow the fastest in the coming decade. Overall, discretionary spending is expected to grow by just over 10% per year to reach $51.3 billion in 2015.

Table 4.4
Key Discretionary Expenditure of the Mass Affluent

Key discretionary Expenditure Items (2004 US$ billion)	2005	2015	Average annual growth
Dining and Entertaining	$5.3	$8.0	4.2%
Shopping	$5.6	$14.4	12.0%
Travel & Leisure	$3.3	$13.6	15.2%
Private Health & Luxury Medicine	$1.8	$6.4	13.6%
Automobiles, PCs & Mobile Phones, etc.	$2.8	$8.9	12.3%
Total	$18.8	$51.3	10.6%

(MasterCard Asia/Pacific)

For the rich households, the breakdown of their spending on key discretionary expenditures is summarized in Table 4.5. For them, spending on private health and luxury medicine, and on travel and leisure activities will be the fastest growing, estimated at 17% and 16.5% per year, respectively. The estimated 400,000 households in the "rich" category will command $11 billion of discretionary spending in 2015.

Table 4.5

Key Discretionary Expenditure of the Rich

Key discretionary Expenditure Items (2004 US$ billion)	2005	2015	Average annual growth
Dining and Entertaining	$0.9	$2.0	8.3%
Shopping	$0.9	$3.6	15.0%
Travel & Leisure	$0.5	$2.3	16.5%
Private Health & Luxury Medicine	$0.3	$1.4	17.0%
Automobiles, PCs & Mobile Phones, etc.	$0.5	$1.7	13.5%
Total	$3.1	$11.0	13.5%

MasterCard Asia/Pacific

What are these mass affluent and rich like as consumers? Given their very diverse backgrounds and the intricate intertwining of their pathways to affluence, their consumption behavior undoubtedly spans the spectrum from the *nouveau riche* to the sophisticated and refined. As described earlier, there are families with a history of wealth stretching back over a hundred years and four or five generations. For these families there is plenty of time to acquire refinement and sophistication. On the other hand, first generation pioneering entrepreneurs, especially those from humbler beginnings, may want to advertise their wealth as loudly and conspicuously as possible. In between, the swelling ranks of the mass affluent drawn from the well educated may exhibit a level of sophistication and subtlety as consumers not typically associated with their relatively new status of affluence. This is because higher education often, though not necessarily, provides a level of "polishing" that could not be acquired otherwise. Given this wide range of consumer behavior, there is clearly ample scope for segmentation and niche marketing. The bottom line is that this is a rapidly expanding and multifaceted high-end consumer market, with plenty of exciting opportunities for all.

The media is fond of referring to Australia as the "lucky country" because of its steady economic growth for the past decade and a half. The fact is that luck has little to do with Australia's enviable track record. Structural reform and market liberalization have fundamentally transformed Australia's economy in the past 20 years, just in time to put it in a position to benefit from the current wave of globalization. Productivity growth has averaged over 3% per year in the past 15 years, raising Australia's per capita GDP ranking from 15th in 1985, to seventh in 2003 among OECD countries.[1]

Structural reform has reduced the effective rate of manufacturing assistance and tariff protection, for example, from 22% of cost of production in 1985, to 4% in 2003. The result is that Australian manufacturers have become more efficient and competitive overseas. As illustrated in Chart 5.1, Australian exports as a percentage of GDP grew from 15% in 1985, to 23% in 2003; and from 17% to 20% for imports.

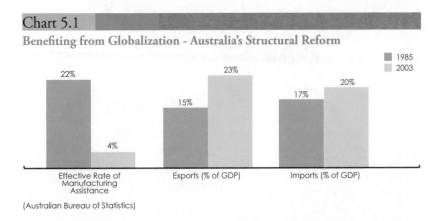

Chart 5.1
Benefiting from Globalization - Australia's Structural Reform

(Australian Bureau of Statistics)

Australian exports have been most successful in penetrating the dynamic markets in East and Southeast Asia. As summarized in Table 5.1, Australia's export growth to the US has actually slowed in recent years, as indicated by the contrast between average annual growth rates over the 2001-2004 period with the 1993-2004 period. Comparisons between these two periods for Japan, China and Thailand, however, show that export growth to these markets has accelerated.

Table 5.1
Australia's Rising Exports to Asia

Average annual growth rate of export to:	1993 - 2004	2001 - 2004
World	6.5%	8.5%
EU	5.1%	7.9%
US	12.0%	3.2%
Japan	4.0%	7.4%
China	17.2%	22.8%
Thailand	11.2%	20.4%

(IMF merchandise trade data)

The success of Australia's external sector is a direct reflection of its internal transformation. Business conditions have vastly improved for small private entrepreneurs. As Table 5.2 shows, small businesses (defined as those employing less than 20 people) have grown from accounting for 94% of total business establishments in 1984, to 96% in 2004. Some 175,000 new small businesses were formed in 2004, compared with about 74,500 in 1984. More important is that a greater number of the new businesses formed are in the skills- and knowledge-intensive areas. For example, only 10.7% were in business services in 1985; in 2004, this increased to account for 17% of all small businesses. In the education sector, small businesses grew from 1.4% of total to 2.2%; and similarly, finance sector small businesses increased from 1.3% of total to 1.5%.

Table 5.2

Australia's Rising Entrepreneurs

	1984	2004
Small business as % of all businesses	94%	96%
New small business formation	74,484	175,282
Small business in business services as % of total new small business	10.7%	17.0%
Small business in education services as % of total new small business	1.4%	2.2%
Small business in the finance sector as % of total new small business	1.3%	1.5%

(Australia Bureau of Statistics, Small Business in Australia, 2005)

Many small businesses in high-tech and high-end services are set up to engage the global market. Some 87% of all Australian exporters in 2005 are those with annual revenue of less than one million Australian dollars. In fact, about 16,600 small businesses export less than $100,000 each per year.[2] These are businesses run by entrepreneurs with globally competitive products and services which can successfully access overseas markets wherever they can be found. This is a powerful indication of the revival of Australia's entrepreneurial energy, which is adding dynamism to the economy in general, and widening the pioneering pathway to affluence, especially for the younger and better educated Australians.

The dynamism in the pioneering pathway to affluence is complemented by the inheritance pathway and the professional pathway. In many instances, the inheritance pathway enables the would-be entrepreneur to get a good education because of financial support from the family, and then in the form of seed capital. Family connections in the right places also help. The professional pathway, on the other hand, remains important as well-paid professional employment continues to be a primary means for the well-educated and skilled Australians to join the rank of the mass affluent.

THE INHERITANCE PATHWAY TO AFFLUENCE

As a society that prides itself on its egalitarian tradition, Australia does not really have many family-owned business dynasties that go back for generations. The richest man in Australia, however, is indeed an heir to a family fortune. James Packer, son of the late Kerry Packer, inherited the bulk of his father's assets when the elder Packer died in December 2005. The elder Packer left behind controlling stakes in the media empire Publishing & Broadcasting (PBL), which owned the Nine Television Network, scores of magazines, a 25% stake in New Regency Films, as well as significant equity in Challenger Financial Services and Consolidated Pastoral. James Packer also has invested in gaming projects in Macau. He is said to have net assets worth some $5 billion.[3]

Another well-known case is the retail business John Gandel inherited from his Polish immigrant parents. He used the inheritance, however, as a stepping stone for his own pioneering entrepreneurial endeavor. Gandel sold the retail business and built his own successful business in property development, including shopping centers. In early 2005, he bought a 50% stake in an Israeli water irrigation company. He is said to be worth $1.4 billion.[4]

These are, of course, the "superstars" of inherited fortunes. For most Australians, the inheritance pathway to affluence operates in much more modest fashion. As suggested earlier, a good but expensive education is often critical. Seed capital from the family is also extremely useful for young entrepreneurs with little savings and not yet able to attract outside investment or venture capital. In this regard, the inheritance pathway is an important component to make the pioneering pathway to affluence work more effectively.

THE PIONEERING PATHWAY TO AFFLUENCE

One high-profile self-made Australian billionaire is Frank Lowy, yet another immigrant who started his working life running deli restaurants. He succeeded fabulously in his commercial property investment, and, at last count, owned some 130 shopping malls in Australia, New Zealand, the UK and the US under the Westfield name. His net assets are in the billions of dollars. He is also the chairman of the Football Federation of Australia, and has funded the establishment of the Lowy Institute for International Policy, a private think tank. His three sons are all involved in the business.

Lowy's is just one high-profile pioneering success in an immigrant society that values its rugged individualism. This longstanding feature of the Australian society has benefited from the market liberalization in the past two decades, which has created a more welcoming environment for entrepreneurial startups. The new global business environment, animated by the growth of the internet and e-commerce, is also more conducive for entrepreneurs that aim to sell globally without being handicapped by their small size. Many of these entrepreneurs will certainly succeed in the coming decade in joining the rank of the mass affluent and the rich.

THE PROFESSIONAL PATHWAY TO AFFLUENCE

Australia's large service economy requires highly skilled professionals of all kinds-from medical doctors to financial analysts to personal fitness consultants and trainers. These professions offer a pathway to affluence as many of them, at least at a certain senior level, are well paid enough for qualifying for the mass affluent, defined as annual household income of $100,000 to $250,000. Australia's education system is also up to the task for producing well trained graduates with the requisite standards and skills to enter these professions.

In 2005, only about 10% of the labor force had university degrees; another 15% were qualified for specific trades; 20% had post-secondary certificates or diplomas, and 16% were secondary school graduates. In 2015, it is projected that the proportion of university graduates will rise to 20% of the labor force, a significant increase. Those who are trade qualified will increase to 21% of the labor force. In contrast, the portion holding post-secondary certificates or diplomas will drop to 8% of the labor force. Secondary-school graduates will also increase to 23% of the labor force. The overall picture is that the labor force will be much better educated than it is today. This will enhance the professional pathway to affluence to enable many more Australians to join at least the rank of the mass affluent, if not the rich.

Table 5.3

Labor Force Education Profile

Education level	2005	2015 projections
University Degree	12%	20%
Trade Qualification	15%	21%
Certificate/Diploma	20%	8%
Secondary	16%	23%

(Australia Bureau of Statistics)

SIZE AND SPENDING POWER OF THE MASS AFFLUENT AND THE RICH

How big is the mass affluent consumer market today, and in 10 years' time? It is estimated that in 2005 there were just over 300,000 households with annual income between $100,000 and $250,000, accounting for 4.1% of total households in Australia. Their average income was $143,000, and collectively they earned $43.5 billion in income. Assuming a conservative trend rate of real GDP growth of 3.5% per year, it is expected that by 2015 there will be 425,000 households in the mass affluent category, accounting for 5.2% of total households in Australia. Their average annual income is estimated at $145,000, not much higher than what it was in 2005. Collectively, however, their income will reach $61.4 billion.

Table 5.4

Size and Income of the Mass Affluent

Annual income $100,000 to $250,000 (2004 US$ exchange rate)	2005	2015	Average annual growth
Number of Households	305,000	425,000	3.9%
Total Household Income	$43.5 billion	$61.4 billion	4.1%
Average Annual Household Income	$143,000	$145,000	0.1%

(MasterCard Worldwide, Asia/Pacific)

What about the "rich" households, defined as those with annual income exceeding $250,000? It is estimated that in 2005 there were 76,800 such households in Australia, accounting for just over 1% of total households. Their average annual income was a sizable $347,000. The size of the rich households is expected to increase to almost 119,000 in 2015, which will account for 1.5% of total households at that time. Their average annual income will also be slightly higher at $351,000 per household. Collectively their income that year will be $41.7 billion.

Table 5.5

Size and Income of the Rich

Annual income > $250,000 (constant 2004 US$)	2005	2015	Average annual growth
Number of Households	76,800	118,850	5.5%
Total Household Income	$26.7 billion	$41.7 billion	5.7%
Average Annual Household Income	$347,000	$351,000	0.1%

(MasterCard Worldwide, Asia/Pacific)

At the apex of these rich households are 35 of Australia's richest families. A breakdown of the industries in which they own most of their assets is shown in Chart 5.2, and provides an interesting picture of their business interests. Over one-third, 39%, made their fortunes in real estate, a direct reflection of the transformation of Australia from a resource-based economy into an urban service economy in the last several decades. Surprisingly, 15% have their main assets in the media and, not surprisingly, 10% in mining, which reflects Australia's traditional strength in resources. Another 10% is in logistics, reflecting the importance of transportation and communications links due to the country's massive land mass and widely dispersed population.

Chart 5.2

Industry Sectors of the richest families in Australia (2005)

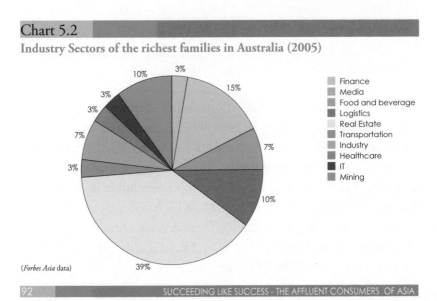

Finance
Media
Food and beverage
Logistics
Real Estate
Transportation
Industry
Healthcare
IT
Mining

(*Forbes Asia* data)

From the perspective of discretionary spending, the mass affluent households on average spent $18,500 in 2005, and the rich households spent over $50,000. Their discretionary spending will grow slowly over the next decade, reaching $21,000 for the mass affluent households, and $62,000 for the rich households.

Table 5.6

Discretionary Spending Estimates

Per Household Discretionary Spending (constant 2004 US$)	2005	2015	Average annual growth
The Mass Affluent	$18,500	$21,000	1.3%
The Rich	$50,500	$62,000	2.1%

(MasterCard Worldwide, Asia/Pacific)

When broken down into the five key discretionary expenditure items, spending on travel and related leisure activities is the highest for the mass affluent households, followed by dining and entertaining. This pattern is expected to hold for the next 10 years. By 2015, their collective discretionary spending on these five key expenditures will reach an impressive $18.5 billion.

Table 5.7

Key Discretionary Expenditure of the Mass Affluent

Key discretionary Expenditure Items (2004 US$ billion)	2005	2015	Average annual growth
Dining and Entertaining	$3.2	$4.4	3.7%
Shopping	$2.4	$3.3	3.9%
Travel & Leisure	$3.9	$5.7	5.0%
Private Health & Luxury Medicine	$0.7	$1.1	5.3%
Automobiles, PCs & Mobile Phones, etc.	$2.6	$3.9	4.9%
Total	$12.9	$18.5	4.3%

(MasterCard Asia/Pacific)

The rich households appear to have a similar spending pattern in their discretionary expenditures as the mass affluent. In 2015, the 119,000 rich households will command $12.5 billion worth of discretionary spending power.

Table 5.8
Key Discretionary Expenditure of the Rich

Key discretionary Expenditure Items (2004 US$ billion)	2005	2015	Average annual growth
Dining and Entertaining	$2.0	$3.0	5.2%
Shopping	$1.5	$2.3	5.4%
Travel & Leisure	$2.4	$3.9	6.2%
Private Health & Luxury Medicine	$0.5	$0.8	6.9%
Automobiles, PCs & Mobile Phones, etc.	$1.6	$2.6	6.5%
Total	$7.9	$12.5	5.9%

(MasterCard Asia/Pacific)

The mass affluent and the rich households combined will have a massive $31 billion worth of discretionary spending power in 2015. This impressive amount of purchasing power, however, will likely to be spent in ways that are inconspicuous and understated. The same rugged individualism that characterizes the Australian society also means that most people are not likely to be impressed by loud and showy consumption styles. Old-fashioned virtues like substance, quality and good value for money are more likely to be the winning features in this high-end consumer market than flashy designs and ostentatious demonstrations of wealth.

AFFLUENT CONSUMERS OF KOREA, TAIWAN AND HONG KONG 6

Korea, Taiwan and Hong Kong are three of the original East Asian "tigers"[1] that successfully industrialized and grew rapidly in the last four decades, raising themselves from poverty to rank among the world's leading economic powerhouses. Between 1960 and 2005, per capita nominal GDP rose by 90 times in Korea, 88 times in Taiwan, and over 90 times in Hong Kong. While the 1997 crisis dented their high growth rates for a few years and exposed some of their structural weaknesses, all have since recovered, and reforms were quickly implemented. All are continuing on their paths to higher income and expanding prosperity. The most prosperous of their population, the mass affluent and the rich households, are set to increase in size and purchasing power in the next decade, making Korea, Taiwan and Hong Kong even more attractive as high-end consumer markets.

General Park Chung-hee seized power in a military coup in 1961, impatient with the apparent lack of progress of the civilian government in raising economic growth and building a stronger defense to counter the threat from the communist North. Park was a tough soldier, born in poverty and serving as a young man in the Japanese military in Manchuria. Having survived the brutality of Japanese military life and wars, he was single-mindedly committed to industrializing Korea as fast as he could. He was subsequently dubbed the first CEO of Korea Inc.

Park was supported by young and energetic military officers who shared the same goals of economic growth and nation-building. They started to gather around them a core group of highly competent technocrats, and a national strategy began to take shape. It was based on what they could see immediately with their own eyes—the rise of Japan. It also helped that many of the young Koreans at that time were educated in Japanese institutions and were familiar with Japan's postwar economic revival, even if many of them harbored anti-Japanese sentiments. Promoting labor-intensive manufacturing and exports became the first step.

As growth started to pick up momentum, Park and his senior economic advisors came to the conclusion, a momentous one as subsequent events show, that in order for Korea to be truly successful in the global market, they needed big and strong companies. So they set themselves the task of identifying and building up national "champions" in industries who could lead Korea to succeed in the global market. Park and his advisors selected companies that had showed initial success, often companies set up by tough, confident and aggressive entrepreneurs. These companies were then supported by the government with low-interest loans, tax concessions and other preferential treatments to assist them to expand. They became known as the *chaebols*—large business groups that had diversified operations in many industries, and were run and controlled by a founding family. The most successful of these are now well-known: Samsung, LG and Hyundai.

Heavy industry was an obsession with Park because of the ever-present invasion threat from the communist North. Capability in modern armament production requires well developed heavy industries. In the 1970s, he pushed through a program to target six heavy industries: steel, petrochemical, nonferrous metals, ship building, electronics and machinery. *Chaebols* were encouraged to move aggressively into these industries, all of them requiring large economies of scale to be efficient. With generous credits, government contracts and protection in the domestic market, the chaebols succeeded beyond expectation. A highly disciplined work force was also a tremendous plus.

The *chaebols* became fabulously rich in these decades of head-long growth. By mid-1970s, the government was beginning to scale back its intervention. More market friendly policies were introduced by a new generation of technocrats with economics Ph.D.s minted in leading American universities. Then Park was assassinated in 1979 by his own security chief in murky circumstances. Another general took power, then another. While continuing the economic policy of rapid industrial development, the government slowly relaxed its grip on both the economy and society, becoming steadily less autocratic.[2]

The real break came in the aftermath of the 1997 crisis when the post-crisis election brought to power a former dissident and veteran opposition leader Kim Dae-jung. Kim had been jailed and kidnapped by previous governments, had narrowly escaped assassination attempts, and been exiled overseas. He was in his 70s when he became Korea's president, presiding over a country plunged in economic crisis. He was, in many ways, the ideal president for the time. He had had a life-long preparation for this role. He owed no political debts to any vested interests, and he had no plan for a second term. His moral authority alone enabled him to rally the country around him and set a program of market liberalization to restructure the economy and loosen the grip of the *chaebols*, while keeping the militant labor unions in line. Within months the economy started to recover. In 1999, the Korean economy grew by 11%; foreign reserve exceeded $95 billion by 2001, and Korea was able to repay the IMF emergency loans ahead of schedule that year. Thus, Korea engineered rapid industrialization and economic growth under a military dictatorship, and then accomplished a peaceful transition to democracy, accompanied by market liberalization and structural reform, under conditions of an economic crisis. It was no mean feat.

THE PIONEERING PATHWAY TO AFFLUENCE

As the historical background of the *chaebols* suggests, Korea's successful pioneering entrepreneurs worked hand-in-glove almost from the beginning with the government. The story of the founder of Hyundai, Chung Ju-yung, is a case in point. Born in a poor village in today's North Korea, Chung moved to Seoul in the 1930s and eked out a living working as a laborer. Then he set himself up as a construction contractor, taking on small projects. The projects got bigger when he got contracts from the US military and the South Korean government during and after the Korean War. That was when he met General Park. Legend has it that Chung was contracted to build a section of Korea's new cross-country highway. General Park, as was his custom, liked to visit work sites unannounced by helicopter. One day he arrived at Chung's work site uninvited at dawn only to find Chung was already hard at work alongside his workers. Impressed, Park befriended Chung and rewarded him with bigger contracts. Then he asked Chung if he knew anything about cars. This question led to the launch of Hyundai Motors in 1967. Five years later Hyundai launched its first shipyard. After that it was on its way to becoming a heavy industry powerhouse.

Like Chung, Lee Byung-chul is another self-made entrepreneur who founded the *chaebol* Samsung. It is now Korea's largest industrial conglomerate. At its heart is Samsung Electronics, accounting for close to a fifth of Korea's exports. Like Chung, Lee's story is one of sheer determination, raw ambition and a great deal of hard work. Samsung also grew big on the back of government patronage.

Unlike the industrial *chaebols*, Shin Kyuk-ho, an 85-year-old billionaire, built his fortune in food and retail. He founded the giant

Lotte Confectionery which is now estimated to be an empire of some $26 billion in assets. Shin began as a small, humble maker of chewing gum in 1948, and it was in retail and fast food that he excelled, as opposed to shipyards and electronics. He gradually expanded the Lotte Group into hotels, department stores and amusement parks, benefiting from the rise of Koreans' general living standards and purchasing power. Fast paced urbanization facilitated his property development business. Lotte Shopping has become Korea's most successful department store. The octogenarian Shin has not slowed down one bit—he is now busy planning Lotte's expansion into Russia, China and Southeast Asia.

The success of the *chaebols* in turn created new business opportunities for a later generation of entrepreneurs to become independent suppliers to them. So their pioneering efforts nurtured other pioneers that came after them. The close relations of the *chaebols* with previous military governments (which some critics have charged as corrupt collusions) have come back to haunt some of their founders as in the case of Daewoo and Hyundai. The 1997 crisis also trimmed their vaulting ambitions, bringing them back to earth. In fact many second- and third-tier *chaebols* did not survive. However, their impact on the Korean society, especially in blazing a path to affluence, remains very real and ever-present.

THE PROFESSIONAL PATHWAY TO AFFLUENCE

The professional pathway to affluence was opened up by the *chaebols* as technical and better paid employment gradually expanded. How Woo Doo-myung's and Kim Tae-yong's lives were changed in the past 30 years illustrates this process. Woo Doo-myung turned 58 in 2006. He joined Hyundai in 1972 and was immediately assigned to the team building the company's first oil tanker in the southern coastal town of Ulsan. Shipbuilding was in its infancy in Korea and no one had built anything like what Hyundai was trying to do. Woo and fellow workers actually had difficulty reading the blueprints as they were so new to the business. They worked routinely 17 hours a day to try to stay on schedule. Woo remembers that one day

Hyundai's founder Chung came to the dockside and promised the workers that they all would have a TV and a refrigerator in five years, and a car in 15. It was like promising them the moon. Woo was earning $360 a year at that time.

In two years Hyundai completed its first oil tanker on time and below budget. Woo and fellow workers felt immensely proud, and Chung celebrated with them by hosting a feast on a hill overlooking the grimy industrial harbor of Ulsan. Thirty years later, it turns out that Chung's promise was a major understatement. Woo is still with Hyundai, in charge of shipyard safety training. His salary and annual bonus together more than qualify him as a member of the mass affluent, defined as those earning between $75,000 and $200,000 a year. He owns a large apartment and both he and his wife own a car. His two children are both medical doctors.

Kim Tae-yong, who turned 50 in 2006, came from Ulsan where Hyundai has its shipyard and auto works. Kim grew up in a farming family with six brothers and sisters. The whole family lived in a mud hut, and when not at school Kim worked in the fields barefoot in hand-me-down clothes. He still remembers seeing a massive ship being launched by Hyundai and how enthralled he was at the sight. Working with gleaming machinery seemed like being in a wonderland compared with traditional farming. He aimed there and then to work for Hyundai when he grew up.

His wish came true after he completed high school and his compulsory military service. He joined Hyundai Motors and was trained to check car quality on the assembly line. He thought that was the best job in the world. His opinion has not changed 27 years later. He is still with Hyundai Motors, except in a more senior managerial position. He just bought a new four-bedroom apartment. He has a large TV and a piano in his living room and a luxury sedan in the parking lot. Like Woo, his salary and annual bonus qualify him as a member of Korea's mass affluent.[3]

For younger and well-educated Koreans, the professional pathway to affluence is a well trodden one today. The high-end service economy is creating more well-paid employment. Better educational opportunities are enabling more young Koreans to qualify for these jobs, thus joining the rank of the mass affluent and, occasionally, even the rich. But it all began with Woo Doo-myung's and Kim Tae-yong's generation and their journey from rags to riches.

THE INHERITANCE PATHWAY TO AFFLUENCE

The *chaebols* are also Korea's family dynasties. Chung Mong-kyu, founder Chung Ju-yong's grand nephew, for example, became the chairman of Hyundai Motors in 1996 at the age of 33. Lee Kun-hee, third son of Samsung founder Lee Byung-chul, took over the running of the business in 1987. An exception is the founder of Daewoo, Kim Woo-choong. He explicitly forbade his two sons to be groomed to take over the business. One of the sons became an architect, the other a professional golfer. Given the fate of Daewoo after the 1997 crisis (it collapsed), Kim's decision was a blessing in disguise for his sons. These successions are, however, often accompanied by bitter battles fought among family members.

The much more far-reaching way in which the inheritance pathway functions is for many middle-class Korean families to "endow" their children with a higher education, often paying the costs (high for the average Korean middle-class family) of attending universities overseas in the US and the UK. Thus prepared, their children stand a much better chance to enter into well paid professional employment and to go on their way to joining the mass affluent and the rich.

MARKET SIZE OF THE MASS AFFLUENT AND THE RICH

It is estimated that in 2005 there were over 600,000 households with annual income of between $75,000 and $200,000, accounting for 3.8% of total households. By 2015, assuming a conservative trend rate of real GDP growth of 4.5% per year in the next 10 years, it is expected that there will be just over 1.5 million households that qualify for being in the rank of mass affluent. This will amount to 8% of total households in 2015, and a strong indicator of expanding prosperity. By then these households will collectively have an impressive annual income of over $174 billion. Their average income per household should be largely unchanged in real terms between 2005 and 2015, rising only very marginally from $113,200 per household to $115,600 per household.

Table 6.1
Size and Income of the Mass Affluent

Annual income $75,000 to $200,000 (2004 US$ exchange rate)	2005	2015	Cumulative annual growth
Number of Households	613,300	1,509,000	9.4%
Total Household Income	$69.4 billion	$174.4 billion	9.6%
Average Annual Household Income	$113,200	$115,600	0.2%

(MasterCard Worldwide, Asia/Pacific)

The rich households, defined as those earning more than $200,000 per year, were estimated to number 159,000 in 2005, accounting for just 1% of total households. By 2015, they are expected to increase to 542,000, the result of an impressive 13% growth per year, and will account for 2.9% of total households.

Table 6.2
Size and Income of the Rich

Annual income > $200,000 (constant 2004 US$)	2005	2015	Cumulative annual growth
Number of Households	159,000	542,000	13.0%
Total Household Income	$47.1 billion	$168.3 billion	13.6%
Average Annual Household Income	$297,000	$311,000	0.5%

(MasterCard Worldwide, Asia/Pacific)

As summarized in Table 6.3, the average discretionary spending per year of the mass affluent households was estimated at $22,600 in 2005, and will be $28,900 in 2015. For the rich households, it was an impressive $74,300 in 2005, rising to an estimated $87,000 in 2015.

Table 6.3

Discretionary Spending Estimates

Per Household Discretionary Spending (constant 2004 US$)	2005	2015	Cumulative annual growth
The Mass Affluent	$22,600	$28,900	2.5%
The Rich	$74,300	$87,000	1.6%

(MasterCard Worldwide, Asia/Pacific)

Dining and entertaining is the biggest discretionary expenditure item for the mass affluent households. But the fastest growing is travel and related leisure activities. Collectively, their five key discretionary expenditures will come to $36.4 billion in 2015.

Table 6.4

Key Discretionary Expenditure of the Mass Affluent

Key discretionary Expenditure Items (2004 US$ billion)	2005	2015	Cumulative annual growth
Dining and Entertaining	$6.2	$12.1	6.9%
Shopping	$3.2	$7.6	9.0%
Travel & Leisure	$2.3	$5.6	9.3%
Private Health & Luxury Medicine	$1.0	$2.1	7.7%
Automobiles, PCs & Mobile Phones, etc.	$4.0	$9.0	8.5%
Total	$16.7	$36.4	8.1%

(MasterCard Worldwide, Asia/Pacific)

Similar to the mass affluent households, dining and entertaining is the biggest discretionary expenditure item for the rich households. Shopping, however, is the fastest growing expenditure item for them. By 2015, the rich households of Korea are expected to spend over $35 billion on these five discretionary expenditure items.

Table 6.5
Key Discretionary Expenditure of the Rich

Key discretionary Expenditure Items (2004 US$ billion)	2005	2015	Cumulative annual growth
Dining and Entertaining	$4.2	$11.8	10.8%
Shopping	$2.1	$7.4	13.4%
Travel & Leisure	$1.6	$5.4	12.9%
Private Health & Luxury Medicine	$0.7	$2.1	11.6%
Automobiles, PCs & Mobile Phones, etc.	$2.7	$8.6	12.3%
Total	$11.3	$35.3	12.1%

(MasterCard Worldwide, Asia/Pacific)

TAIWAN

Taiwan's postwar march to prosperity started out in even less promising circumstances than those of Korea's. In 1949, the communist-led forces over-ran the mainland of China, decisively defeating the forces of the Nationalist Government (Kuomintang) led by Chiang Kai-shek. Upward of two million Kuomintang officials, soldiers and their families fled to Taiwan. The communist forces were stopped by the Taiwan Strait, not having the naval capability to cross it to mount an amphibious assault. Ever since then Beijing has called Taiwan a "renegade province," and vows to "reunify" it with the rest of China.

On the island of Taiwan, Chiang set up his Nationalist government and braced himself for the expected communist assault. The Seventh Fleet of the US Navy intervened, however, and shielded Taiwan with a protective screen. Chiang and his close advisors meantime took a long hard look at what went wrong on the mainland and then took stock of what they had to do. They concluded unequivocally that economic mismanagement and endemic corruption were the real causes of defeat; and rapid industrialization and economic growth must be achieved in Taiwan if they were to survive.

What followed was a remarkable transformation of Taiwan in the next decades from a dirt-poor island with hardly any resources and a per capita income of about $100 in 1949, to a dynamic economic powerhouse with a per capita income of around $15,000 in 2005. Taiwan's economic planners knew that strong government actions were needed to initiate the process of rapid industrialization, but they were also very conscious of the need to create conditions conducive for entrepreneurs to flourish. They therefore focused on infrastructure development, provisions of health and education, and institutional frameworks to protect private property rights and build an efficient legal system. One very basic but important resource that was at their disposal was a relatively well-educated population. For 50 years beginning in 1895 Taiwan was a Japanese colony; and one of the legacies left from that period was a strong emphasis on education. In 1949, half of the population of Taiwan was literate, a rare situation in most of Asia at that time. Promotion of labor-intensive manufacturing was made easier with a literate workforce. It was made easier still by government policies that provided tax concessions, export subsidies; and heavy investment in improving public infrastructure.[4]

Many well-educated Taiwanese who were living overseas started to return to Taiwan to invest and work. Remarkably Taiwan managed to turn the "brain drain" phenomenon that plagues so many developing countries into a "brain bank" for its development. World-class scientists, engineers and other professionals returned to Taiwan to work for the government, join large corporations, or start their own businesses. At one point in the 1970s, Taiwan could boast of having the highest number of cabinet members with Ph.D. degrees.

Chiang Kai-shek nevertheless ruled with an iron fist. His government was unmistakably authoritarian. He died in 1975, a year before Mao's death in 1976. In the quarter century before his death, Chiang oversaw a sustained period of robust growth and development that put Taiwan among the leading economic performers in Asia, while Mao brought about one economic catastrophe after another. Chiang Ching-kuo, Chiang Kai-shek's son, became president of Taiwan for the next 10 years.

In 1988, shortly before his own death, Chiang Ching-kuo returned Taiwan to democracy. The Nationalist Party appointed Lee Teng-hui, a former agricultural economist educated at Cornell University, to be president. Significantly he was a native Taiwanese, not a mainlander.[5] In 1996, he was re-elected in a free and contested election. Democracy became firmly consolidated in Taiwan after that point.

THE PIONEERING PATHWAY TO AFFLUENCE

Taiwan's government went to extraordinary lengths to "promote" entrepreneurship. When US financial assistance became available for building a chemical plant, the government decided that they needed a businessman to run it. Through its overseas network of contacts, a name came through with strong endorsement and recommendations, Y.C. Wang. An entrepreneur with only a primary school education, Wang had succeeded in several business start-ups. He was actually working in Japan in the lumber business when the Taiwanese government contacted him. He was persuaded to return to Taiwan to take on the job of building Taiwan's chemical industry from scratch. The result is the remarkable success of the Formosa Plastics Group. Wang turned 90 in 2006. He has presided over Formosa Plastics' move from success to success, which now encompasses products in semiconductors, high-value-added specialty plastic products, and even involvement in the research and development of electric cars.

Other examples of well-known first-generation entrepreneurs include Stan Shih, founder of Acer Computers, and his friend Dr. Morris Chang, founder of the Taiwan Semiconductor Manufacturing

Co. (TSMC). Dr. Chang (who was also overseas when the government "recruited" him) founded TSMC with government assistance in 1987, and is known as the "father" of Taiwan's semiconductor industry. Today, TSMC and its rival, United Microelectronics Corp. (UMC), are the world's leading chip foundries.

A successful pioneering entrepreneur of a younger generation is Terry Gou, 57 years old in 2006. He made his fortune in assembling components in manufacturing PCs, mobile phones and MP3 players. His company, Hon Hai Precision, is now one of the world's leading contract manufacturers in consumer electronics. He listed the company in Hong Kong in 2004. He reportedly chose to receive an annual salary of only one New Taiwan dollar (3 US cents) from the company.

In all instances where the government played an active role in launching new industries or setting new companies, it had always been very conscientious in letting private entrepreneurs take the lead while providing selective and judicious financial, technological and marketing support. This approach is a unique and distinctive feature of Taiwan's industrial policy. One lasting legacy of allowing entrepreneurs to play a leading role is the thriving small and medium size business sector in Taiwan. The entrepreneurial business leaders of the large companies were very bottom-line and profit conscious, and they sought to outsource production to smaller and cheaper suppliers wherever possible. Hence, from the beginning, Taiwan's industrialization strongly stimulated the development of a small and medium size business sector that supplies the large companies. In time, many of these medium-size businesses in turn outsourced some of their production to even smaller suppliers, further boosting the growth of the sector. Taiwan's famous ability to adjust production to changing demand conditions stems precisely from having such a dynamic small and medium size business sector.

THE INHERITANCE PATHWAY TO AFFLUENCE

Some of Taiwan's leading businesses are now run by second generation heirs of the founding families. For example, Daniel Tsai, co-CEO of Fubon Financial Holdings, Taiwan's second largest financial services group, took over from his father and founder of the business Tsai Wan-tsai. Trained as a lawyer and educated at Georgetown University in the US, Daniel Tsai and his brother Richard are bringing new management techniques and organizational innovations to the family business.

Another example is Koo Chen-fu, founder of the Koo Group whose flagship China Trust is Taiwan's largest financial services company; he stepped down in 1989 and turned the rein over to his nephew Jeffrey Koo. Known as "Mr. Taiwan," Jeffrey Koo's ambition is to turn China Trust Bank into a true global Chinese bank. Similarly in 1993, Douglas Tong Hsu took over from his father Hsu Yu-ziang, founder of the Far East Group that operates businesses in IT, hotels, department stores and financial services.

Y.C. Wang's daughter, Cher Wang, has built up her own technology business in partnership with her husband Chen Wen-chi. They control Via Technologies, which designs semiconductors, and High Tech Computer, which makes smart phones. Undoubtedly assisted by her privileged position of being the daughter of a billionaire, Cher Wang has nonetheless blazed her own trail and become very successful in her own right. Her path is one of a mixture of both the inheritance and pioneering pathways.

For the less-privileged Taiwanese, the "inheritance" that benefits the younger generation is increasingly a good education, very often in universities in the US, which opens up the professional pathway to affluence. On the other hand, it is also common for young entrepreneurs to get family support in the form of seed capital to launch their own new business start-ups.

THE PROFESSIONAL PATHWAY TO AFFLUENCE

As in many other markets, a good education helps to open up the professional pathway to affluence in Taiwan. The fact that Taiwan has a longer history of high literacy and strong tertiary education means that the bar is higher. Even entry level positions in professional employment demand a good university degree. The result is an exceptionally well educated and highly skilled workforce. A direct reflection of Taiwan's improving critical mass of technological skills and expertise is in its rising ranking in the world in terms of numbers of patents granted in the US as shown in Table 6.6. In 1990, Taiwan ranked number 11 in the world with 732 patents granted in the US. By 2000, Taiwan's rank rose to being number four in the world, with 4,607 patents granted in the US that year. Many Taiwanese have entered the rank of the mass affluent through well paid professional employment leveraging their strong educational background and technological expertise.

Table 6.6
Taiwan's R&D Capability

	1990	1995	2000
Taiwan's world ranking in no. of patents granted in the US	No. 11	No. 7	No. 4
Number of patents granted	732	1,620	4,607

(Directorate of Budget, Accounting & Statistics)

In the past decade, there has been an additional twist to Taiwan's professional pathway to affluence. Many employment opportunities have opened up on the mainland of China for Taiwanese professionals. Taiwanese companies have been the leading investors in China and they have moved many senior managers from Taiwan to the mainland. In addition, foreign multinationals have also found that Taiwanese professionals are ideal managers for their operations in China, being able to speak the language, being familiar with the culture and customs, yet thoroughly schooled in Western business practices.[6] To date, it is estimated there are over one million Taiwanese working and living on the mainland of China, and many are senior managers and technical professionals employed by both Taiwanese companies as well as foreign multinationals. It appears that Taiwan's professional pathway to affluence now operates both in Taiwan itself as well as in China.

MARKET SIZE OF THE MASS AFFLUENT AND THE RICH

It is estimated that in 2005 there were 177,200 households in the mass affluent category, defined as those earning between $75,000 and

$200,000 per year. They accounted for 2.4% of total households. Assuming a trend rate of real GDP growth of 4% per year in the next 10 years, it is projected that the number of mass affluent households will increase to 253,700 in 2015, accounting for 2.9% of total households. Collectively their total income was estimated at $19.8 billion 2005, and is expected to rise to $28.6 billion, an impressive amount of purchasing power. On a per household basis, their average income is not expected to change much between 2005 and 2015.

Table 6.7

Size and Income of the Mass Affluent

Annual income $75,000 to $200,000 (2004 US$ & exchange rate)	2005	2015	Cumulative annual growth
Number of Households	177,200	253,700	3.6%
Total Household Income	$19.8 billion	$28.6 billion	3.7%
Average Annual Household Income	$111,800	$112,600	0.07%

(MasterCard Worldwide, Asia/Pacific)

For the rich households, defined as those earning more than $200,000 per year, their number will increase from 38,800 in 2005 (0.5% of total households), to 59,500 in 2015 (0.7% of total households). In 2015, these 59,500 households will have a collective income of $17.4 billion, or $293,000 each.

Table 6.8

Size and Income of the Rich

Annual income > $200,000 (constant 2004 US$)	2005	2015	Cumulative annual growth
Number of Households	38,800	59,500	4.3%
Total Household Income	$11.3 billion	$17.4 billion	4.4%
Average Annual Household Income	$290,000	$293,000	0.1%

(MasterCard Worldwide, Asia/Pacific)

Both mass affluent and rich households have very significant discretionary spending power. By 2015, it is estimated that the mass affluent households will have on average over $28,000 worth of discretionary spending per household, and for the average rich household, a very impressive $96,700.

Table 6.9

Discretionary Spending Estimates

Per Household Discretionary Spending (constant 2004 US$)	2005	2015	Cumulative annual growth
The Mass Affluent	$25,900	$28,150	0.8%
The Rich	$87,000	$96,700	1.1%

(MasterCard Worldwide, Asia/Pacific)

Among the five key discretionary expenditures, travel and related leisure activities is the biggest among the mass affluent, and it is also the fastest growing. The mass affluent households will spend close to $10 billion collectively on these five discretionary expenditure items in 2015.

Table 6.10

Key Discretionary Expenditure of the Mass Affluent

Key discretionary Expenditure Items (2004 US$ billion)	2005	2015	Cumulative annual growth
Dining and Entertaining	$1.7	$2.2	2.6%
Shopping	$0.7	$1.0	3.6%
Travel & Leisure	$2.2	$3.5	4.8%
Private Health & Luxury Medicine	$0.9	$1.4	4.5%
Automobiles, PCs & Mobile Phones, etc.	$1.2	$1.8	4.1%
Total	$6.7	$9.9	4.0%

(MasterCard Worldwide, Asia/Pacific)

The rich households exhibit a similar pattern in their discretionary spending. Travel and leisure is the biggest and is expected to have the highest growth rate. By 2015, the rich households of Taiwan will collectively spend close to $7 billion on these five key discretionary expenditures.

Table 6.11
Key Discretionary Expenditure of the Rich

Key discretionary Expenditure Items (2004 US$ billion)	2005	2015	Cumulative annual growth
Dining and Entertaining	$1.0	$1.4	3.4%
Shopping	$0.4	$0.7	5.8%
Travel & Leisure	$1.5	$2.8	6.5%
Private Health & Luxury Medicine	$0.5	$0.9	6.1%
Automobiles, PCs & Mobile Phones, etc.	$0.6	$1.1	6.2%
Total	$4.0	$6.9	5.6%

(MasterCard Worldwide, Asia/Pacific)

HONG KONG

Hong Kong has grown faster and become more prosperous than Korea and Taiwan with a completely different approach in terms of government policy. Under a British colonial administration until 1997, Hong Kong's industrial policy is best described as not having one. Instead of explicit policies for rapid industrialization, the colonial administration focused on maintaining law and order, providing adequate industrial and civil infrastructure, and building an impartial and efficient legal system based on the British model. The result has been described as a dynamic *laissez-faire* free market where entrepreneurs flourished.[7]

While it is Hong Kong's entrepreneurial energy that lifted the once poverty-stricken and slum-ridden city to become a world-class metropolis, it is also the same unfettered entrepreneurial energy that drove its transformation from thriving on labor-intensive manufacturing to a high-end service economy. As shown in Table 6.12, in 1980 services accounted for only 60% of Hong Kong's economy. By 2005, Hong Kong's economy was by and large a service sector economy with services representing 90% of its GDP.

Table 6.12

Hong Kong's Rising Service Sector

	Service sector's share of GDP
1980	60%
2005	90%

(Hong Kong Census & Statistics Department)

More telling are the changes observed in Hong Kong's employment structure. As summarized in Table 6.13, in 1981, manufacturing accounted for 39% of Hong Kong's employment, when its still relatively low wages provided a comparative advantage. By 2004, manufacturing had practically vanished, accounting for only 8% of total employment. Hong Kong entrepreneurs seized the opportunity of China's market opening, especially the new special economic zone just across the border in Shenzhen, to relocate their manufacturing plants there lock, stock and barrel. Rising wages in Hong Kong and rock-bottom wages in China made the decision to move a "no-brainer." The government made no attempt to "protect" or retain the manufacturing sector in Hong Kong. Consequently, Hong Kong has changed rapidly in accordance to its shifting comparative advantage-being a hub of high-end services that caters increasingly to China's needs. As a result, employment in financial and business services (where the best paid jobs are found) expanded from 5% of total employment in 1981, to 18% in 2004.

Table 6.13

Hong Kong's Changing Employment Structure

	1981	2004
Manufacturing	39%	8%
Construction	9%	10%
Transport	8%	11%
Personal Services	18%	22%
Trade & Tourism	21%	31%
Financial & Business Services	5%	18%

(Hong Kong Census & Statistics Department)

A feature of Hong Kong's unfettered entrepreneurial energy is its remarkable resilience. Hong Kong has faced down crisis after crisis, many of which would have sunk a bigger economy. In 1954 and again in 1957 there were riots with pitched battles fought between pro-Taiwan and pro-communist groups. There was a run on banks in 1964, damaging the financial sector. In 1967, the Cultural Revolution raging in China spilt over and Hong Kong was rocked by street demonstrations and strikes by pro-communist labor unions. The energy crisis in 1975 hurt Hong Kong badly. The Sino-British talks on Hong Kong's future in 1982-1984 created serious uncertainty and severely damaged confidence. This was followed by the 1987 stock-market crash. In 1989 there was the fallout of the Tiananmen massacre in Beijing.[8] In every instance, Hong Kong's free market coped with the challenges, adapted and adjusted to the environment, and quickly refocused on the real business at hand: getting rich. It is essentially no different in the post-1997 era. In spite of widespread dissatisfaction with the Beijing-appointed administration, Hong Kong's free market environment has remained remarkably intact. In recent years, there are signs that it has consolidated its position as an investment and financial hub that occupies a uniquely important role in the Chinese economy, the rise of Shanghai notwithstanding.

THE PIONEERING PATHWAY TO AFFLUENCE

Li Ka-shing is the best known and arguably the most important pioneering entrepreneur of Hong Kong. His story is virtually a micro-version of the macro story of Hong Kong. A member of the Teochiu clan (a dialect group), Li was born in southern China in 1928. His father, a school teacher, took the family to Hong Kong in 1940, but died two years later, leaving the teenage Li to fend for himself and to support his mother and two younger siblings. He sold plastic flowers and gadgets like toys and watchbands; and gradually built up a war chest of some $5,000 with which he used to set up his own plastic factory in 1950. He established his company Cheung Kong in the mid-1950s, and then expanded the business into construction, property, infrastructure, retail and telecom. He is known in Hong Kong as "superman," a tribute to his over five decades of business successes. Widely believed to be Asia's richest man and one of the world's top billionaires,[9] his business empire, anchored with his control over the Cheung Kong Group and Hutchison Whampoa, now operates with a global reach from Panama to Canada, and from China to Europe. He is also famous for his philanthropic generosity. He endowed an entire university in Shantou in southern China, ancestral home of the Teochiu clan. In 2005, he made a $25 million donation to Hong Kong University and another multimillion-dollar donation to the University of California, Berkeley.

Another iconic pioneering entrepreneur of Hong Kong is Lee Shau-kee, who founded Henderson Land. The same age as Li Ka-shing, and coming from the same region of southern China, Lee arrived in Hong Kong in 1947, and became a dealer in foreign exchange. In 1956, he and seven partners founded Eternal Enterprises to go into the real estate business. One of the partners was the famous Kwok Tak-sing who later founded Sun Hung Kai Properties, also with Lee as a partner. Lee expanded into utilities, public transport, hotels; but the core business remains property development which by the 1990s included investments in China,

Singapore and North America. He was consistently ranked the richest man in Hong Kong in the 1990s, beating Li Ka-shing, until Li overtook him in the late 1990s.

It is not surprising to find a Hong Kong business tycoon with strong pro-communist inclinations, who in fact made his fortune by assisting Communist China in the early days. Known as the "red capitalist," Henry Fok got started smuggling goods into China during the Korean War when there was a United Nations sanction against China. In the 1960s he helped finance Stanley Ho's casino business in Macau. Then he became a successful real estate developer. By the 1990s he was a leading investor in China, well known for his investment in developing a large and diverse technology park in his native Nansha, located between Guangzhou and Hong Kong. Beijing has never forgotten Fok's help and has always hailed him as a "patriotic capitalist."

These are merely a few iconic entrepreneurial successes in Hong Kong. The fact is Hong Kong's free market environment and extraordinary entrepreneurial energy means rags-to-riches stories are the stable diet of both the tabloid press and case studies in business schools. For every Li Ka-shing there are thousands of successful entrepreneurs, albeit not in the same class. As shown below, Hong Kong has a very large segment of the mass affluent and the rich households, and reputedly has more Rolls Royces per capita than anywhere else in the world.

THE INHERITANCE PATHWAY TO AFFLUENCE

Hong Kong's stock market is one of the largest and most sophisticated in Asia. Yet, a surprisingly high portion of its capitalization belongs to companies that are still family controlled. It has been estimated that companies whose control will be passed from the founding generation to the second generation in the coming years represent about 40% of Hong Kong's stock market index.[10] The inheritance pathway to affluence is set to work over time. Many leading business conglomerates, however, have already gone through the succession process in recent years.

For example, the Kwok brothers, Walter, Thomas and Raymond, took over the management of Sun Hung Kai Properties when their father Kwok Tak-sing died in 1990. Henry Cheng Kar-shun took over from his father Cheng Yu-tung, who founded the New World Development Group and who started by running a successful jewellery store (later an international chain) called Chow Tai Fook Jewellery. In some instances, the second generation heir introduced more professional management style and structure. In other instances, the family business was unsentimentally sold by the younger generation with overseas education and modern management ideas, as when Bernard Chan sold Asia Commercial Bank, a bank started by his grandfather, because it was judged to be a good business deal.[11] The ultimate succession story yet to come is, of course, how Li Ka-shing will pass the control of his business empire to his sons, Victor and Richard. Li turned 78 in 2006, and even though he remains active and appears vigorous, the time will come soon for him to pass on the baton. His two sons have, however, totally different business ideas and management styles; while Victor has stayed close to Li, Richard has struck out on his own in flamboyant style and founded Pacific Century Cyber Work, an internet company. This is no doubt a succession story that Hong Kongers are awaiting with bated breath.

The inheritance pathway is, however, not limited to the passing of the baton from the founding generation to the second generation. In Hong Kong there are family business dynasties that go back many generations. A leading example is Michael Kadoorie, scion of a distinguished Jewish family from Iraq that settled in Asia over a hundred years ago and has become fabulously successful and wealthy. Kadoorie, with his brother-in-law, owns major stakes in the listed Hong Kong and Shanghai Hotels, which operates the famous Peninsula Hotel in Hong Kong, an iconic landmark; as well as China Light and Power Holdings, one of the leading power supply companies in Hong Kong. Kadoorie was knighted by Queen Elizabeth in honor of his extensive charitable and philanthropic activities, among which is his support of the research in the history of Chinese Jews.

THE PROFESSIONAL PATHWAY TO AFFLUENCE

The expansion of Hong Kong's high-end services in recent years has opened up the professional pathway to affluence to more people. As shown in Table 6.13 above, employment in financial and business services now account for 18% of total employment, up from 5% in 1980. This is the employment category where the best paid professional jobs are found. Young and well-educated people in Hong Kong are set to benefit from this development. On the supply side, there are now more institutions of higher education than ever before. For the longest time Hong Kong had only one university, the venerable Hong Kong University, founded in the beginning of the 20th century. Now there is the Chinese University of Hong Kong, the Hong Kong University of Science and Technology, the Hong Kong Baptist University, the City Polytechnic University and others. In the coming years, an increasingly well-educated workforce will send more of its members to join the rank of the mass affluent, and occasionally, the rich.

MARKET SIZE OF THE MASS AFFLUENT AND THE RICH

In 2005, the size of the mass affluent, defined as households with annual income between $100,000 and $250,000, was estimated at 154,000 households, accounting for 7% of Hong Kong's total households. Assuming a trend rate of real GDP growth of 4.5% per year in the next 10 years, the size of the mass affluent is expected to increase to about 252,000, or 10.2% of total households. This compares very favorably with the forecasted 2.4% in Taiwan, and 8% in Korea in 2015. Collectively, the mass affluent households are expected to have a total annual income of almost $37 billion in 2015.

Table 6.14

Size and Income of the Mass Affluent

Annual income $100,000 to $250,000 (2004 US$ & exchange rate)	2005	2015	Cumulative annual growth
Number of Households	154,000	251,700	5.0%
Total Household Income	$22.3 billion	$36.8 billion	5.1%
Average Annual Household Income	$145,000	$147,000	0.07%

(MasterCard Worldwide, Asia/Pacific)

The size of the rich households is estimated to have been 48,500 in 2005, accounting for 2.2% of the total. It is projected to increase to 94,250 in 2015, accounting for 3.8% of the total. Again, this compares very favorably with Taiwan's 0.7% and Korea's 2.9%. This is a direct tribute to the energy of Hong Kong's entrepreneurs and their successes. By 2015, these 94,250 rich households will have a total annual income $34.4 billion.

Table 6.15

Size and Income of the Rich

Annual income > $250,000 (constant 2004 US$)	2005	2015	Cumulative annual growth
Number of Households	48,500	94,250	6.7%
Total Household Income	$17.3 billion	$34.4 billion	7.1%
Average Annual Household Income	$356,600	$365,300	0.2%

(MasterCard Worldwide, Asia/Pacific)

At the apex of these rich households are 17 families whose net worth is in the billions. Consistent with Hong Kong's development history recounted earlier, 46% of their assets are found in the real estate sector, and 0% in manufacturing.

Chart 6.1

Industry Sectors of the richest families in HK (2005)

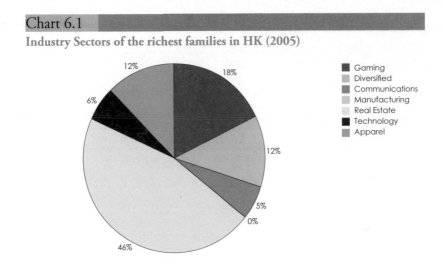

(*Forbes Asia* data)

The discretionary spending of the mass affluent households is estimated to have been $29,000 in 2005, and rising to over $36,000 in 2015. The rich households have much higher average discretionary spending, estimated at $107,600 in 2005, and rising to $120,000 in 2015.

Table 6.16

Discretionary Spending Estimates

Per Household Discretionary Spending (constant 2004 US$)	2005	2015	Cumulative annual growth
The Mass Affluent	$29,000	$36,700	2.4%
The Rich	$107,600	$120,000	1.1%

(MasterCard Worldwide, Asia/Pacific)

Dining and entertaining is the biggest discretionary expenditure item for the mass affluent, and is easy to understand given Hong Kong's fabulous food culture. But it is in travel and leisure activities and in private health and luxury medicine that their spending will grow the fastest. In 2015, it is expected that they will spend some $8.5 billion on these five key discretionary expenditure items.

Table 6.17

Key Discretionary Expenditure of the Mass Affluent

Key discretionary Expenditure Items (2004 US$ billion)	2005	2015	Cumulative annual growth
Dining and Entertaining	$2.3	$3.2	3.4%
Shopping	$1.3	$2.4	6.3%
Travel & Leisure	$0.3	$0.6	7.2%
Private Health & Luxury Medicine	$0.2	$0.4	7.2%
Automobiles, PCs & Mobile Phones, etc.	$1.2	$1.9	4.7%
Total	$5.3	$8.5	4.8%

(MasterCard worldwide, Asia/Pacific)

The rich households have a similar discretionary expenditure pattern as the mass affluent. In their case, however, it is spending on the "automobiles, PCs and mobile phones" category that will grow the fastest. This also makes sense given the penchant of Hong Kong's rich for Rolls Royces and other super luxury cars. In 2015, the forecast is that the rich households will collectively spend $8.5 billion on the five key discretionary expenditures.

Table 6.18

Key Discretionary Expenditure of the Rich

Key discretionary Expenditure Items (2004 US$ billion)	2005	2015	Cumulative annual growth
Dining and Entertaining	$1.8	$3.0	5.2%
Shopping	$1.1	$2.3	7.6%
Travel & Leisure	$0.5	$0.9	6.0%
Private Health & Luxury Medicine	$0.2	$0.4	7.2%
Automobiles, PCs & Mobile Phones, etc.	$0.9	$1.9	7.8%
Total	$4.5	$8.5	6.6%

(MasterCard Worldwide, Asia/Pacific)

Korea, Taiwan and Hong Kong have all achieved rapid economic growth and prosperity through very different development approaches. Korea has depended on the government and industrial policies the most, Taiwan to a much lesser extent, and Hong Kong not at all. Along the same spectrum, it can also be observed that Korea's mass affluent and rich consumers are most conservative, Taiwan's are in between, and Hong Kong's are far more flamboyant, loud and colorful.

Table 6.19

Discretionary Spending in 2015

	Mass affluent	Rich	Total
Korea	$43.6 billion	$47.2 billion	$90.8 billion
Taiwan	$7.1 billion	$5.7 billion	$12.8 billion
Hong Kong	$9.2 billion	$11.3 billion	$20.5 billion
Total of three markets			$124.1 billion

(MasterCard Worldwide, Asia/Pacific)

Differences in their lifestyles and consumption patterns notwithstanding, by 2015 their collective discretionary spending power is estimated at a massive $124 billion. These are truly premium customers in their respective consumer markets.

AFFLUENT CONSUMERS OF SOUTHEAST ASIA: SINGAPORE, MALAYSIA, THAILAND, INDONESIA AND THE PHILIPPINES

7

The five markets covered in this chapter are frequently referred to as the ASEAN-5.[1] In spite of belonging to the same geopolitical grouping, they are very diverse. In population, they range from Indonesia with over 200 million people, to tiny Singapore with 4.3 million people (of which 3.5 million are Singapore citizens and permanent residents). Singapore, however, enjoys the highest income level in the group, with per capita income approaching $30,000, whereas at the opposite end of the spectrum are Indonesia and the Philippines, with per capita income below $2,000.

They also differ greatly in growth dynamics. From the 1960s onward, Singapore has been one of the four East Asian tigers (along with Hong Kong, Korea and Taiwan), recording one of the fastest records of sustained growth in the region. Malaysia, Thailand and Indonesia were the "tiger cubs," achieving high rates of growth until the financial crisis of 1997. Since the crisis, Malaysia's and

Thailand's recoveries have been faster, due to structural reform coupled with a speedy revival of investment and consumption; meanwhile, Indonesia struggled with a succession of ineffective presidents. It was not until President Susilo Bambang Yudhoyono's election in 2004 that serious reform started. The Philippines has been, in contrast, mired in stagnation for decades. Even though it was the least affected by the 1997 crisis, it has also shown itself to be the least capable of shifting to higher growth.

Going further back, their respective pasts are also different. Thailand escaped colonization through a combination of clever diplomacy and effective mobilization of national power. Singapore and Malaysia were parts of British Malaya, and both have inherited the British parliamentary system along with many public institutions in the British mold. Independence was peacefully negotiated during the post-WW II decade. Indonesia, on the other hand, was under a Dutch colonial administration and was granted independence in 1949. The history of the Philippines is more complex as it involves the initial colonization by Spain, then being taken over by the US in 1901. During World War II the Filipino nationalists fought alongside the Americans against the Japanese, and the Philippines was promptly granted independence after the war in 1946. The respective colonial pasts of Southeast Asia (or the lack of, as in the case of Thailand) have left lasting impacts in terms of public institutions, infrastructure development, and the evolution of indigenous social and economic elites.[2]

One common feature shared by these five markets, however, is a strong presence of the overseas Chinese communities. Chinese immigrants started arriving in Southeast Asia more than a thousand years ago. It was, however, in the last 200 years that many of them settled in the region, sinking down local roots. The vast majority of them arrived in 1860 from the south and southeastern coastal regions of China, dominated by five major dialect groups. These are the Hokkien speakers from Fujian province; the Teochiu speakers from an area in northeastern Guangdong province with the county of Shantou being their ancestral home; the Cantonese speakers from Guangzhou, the capital of Guangdong province; the Hakka speakers, who originated in northern China and migrated to the south after the Mongol invasion in the 12th century and settled in parts of Guangdong Province; and finally the Hainanese from Hainan Island, the southernmost province of China.

From the beginning, these dialect groups formed tightly knit networks in Southeast Asia, organized formally as well as informally through guilds, benevolent societies, and village and clan associations. These networks in turn served as commercial linkages that powerfully facilitated their ability to conduct regional trade and raise investment capital without accessing formal financial institutions such as banks. Not being part of indigenous populations, they were able to work closely with local colonial authorities, carving out particular business niches for themselves. These characteristics endowed the overseas Chinese with powerful competitive advantages in business.

In spite of their usually humble origins, they created many wealthy family business empires in Southeast Asia that were passed down from one generation to the next.[3] Cheong Fatt Tze, whose mansion in Penang we visited in chapter one, was the founding patriarch of one such family empire. In the case of Cheong, the business empire did not endure and by the third generation much of the family wealth was gone. As will be seen later, many others have continued to prosper and the younger generations are often the pioneers in reinventing the family business. Thus, a significant portion of the affluent and rich consumers of Southeast Asia today is accounted for by a sizable and prosperous upper-middle class of overseas Chinese origins. At the top, overseas Chinese families are also prominent in owning large business conglomerates and are counted among the richest in the region.

SINGAPORE

Singapore's rise from a third-world trading post to a first-world metropolis is a well-known story. A distinctive feature of Singapore's development is the active role played by the government in engineering structural transformation of the economy in the past five decades. Starting out much like Hong Kong as a location for low-cost and labor-intensive manufacturing, it steadily moved into higher value-added production, bolstered by rapid and impressive public infrastructure development.[4] In recent years, it has repositioned itself as a health sciences hub, a logistics hub and a knowledge hub of higher education. Throughout this process, all three pathways to affluence have functioned effectively to increase the size of both the mass affluent and the rich.

THE INHERITANCE PATHWAY TO AFFLUENCE

As with the rest of the region, Singapore has its share of family business dynasties going back many generations, especially within the overseas Chinese community. In the banking sector, for example, the Oversea-Chinese Banking Corp. (OCBC) is controlled by the Lee family, currently headed by Lee Seng Wee and which started out in agriculture several generations ago. Similarly the United Overseas Bank (UOB) is controlled by another wealthy family of long standing in the region, the Wee family, now headed by Wee Cho Yaw.

In property development, an example of inherited wealth is Kwek Leng Beng, who has expanded the family business successfully to a whole new level. His Millennium & Copthorne Group runs a chain of 90 hotels in 21 countries including the Millennium Resort Scottsdale McCormick Ranch in Arizona and the JW Marriott Hong Kong. His second major company, City Developments, is one of the largest commercial landlords in Singapore. A Ferrari-driving and flamboyant billionaire, Kwek has made headlines in overseas forays such as teaming up with Saudi Arabia's Prince Al Waleed to buy a stake in New York's Plaza Hotel in 1995. A fellow property developer and also heir of a family business is Ong Beng Seng, whose Hotel Properties Ltd. controls a line-up of Four Seasons Hotels in the region, as well as properties in Australia and the UK. (He is actually Malaysian but a long-time resident of Singapore.)

For many Singaporeans who are not in that league, the inheritance most meaningful to them is often family support, as it is for many in Asia. This support is usually for a good university education either in Singapore or abroad, which helps in launching them on the professional pathway to affluence. Seed capital provided by family members is also common as another form of "inheritance" that helps launch young entrepreneurs on their way on the pioneering pathway to affluence.

THE PROFESSIONAL PATHWAY TO AFFLUENCE

The professional pathway to affluence in Singapore functions with two powerful turbocharged engines. The first is the government policy of paying civil servants well. The pay scale is comparable, and occasionally exceeds, that of the corporate sector. Many senior civil servants are able to join the ranks of the mass affluent when reaching a certain level of seniority; and many top government officials easily qualify for the "rich" households on the strength of their regular salary alone.

The second turbocharged engine is Singapore's role as the regional headquarters location for multinational companies. Over 6,000 multinationals have their regional (Asia-wide) or sub-regional (Southeast Asia) headquarters in Singapore. Their presence in turn has generated strong demand for well-paid professionals. For the highly skilled and well educated, of which Singapore's superb education facilities have been providing an ample supply, the professional pathway to affluence is easily accessible. Consequently, the majority of Singapore's mass affluent have come through the professional pathway to affluence.

THE PIONEERING PATHWAY TO AFFLUENCE

In recent years, a consistent message from the government to younger Singaporeans is that they should be more entrepreneurial and creative. Clearly there is a concern that younger Singaporeans are more risk-averse than their elders. If this is true, then Sim Wong Hoo could very well serve as a role model for them. Born in 1955 and the second youngest of 12 children to immigrant parents from China, he indeed had a humble beginning. He graduated with a diploma in electrical engineering from a local college. In 1981 he set up his company, Creative Technology, with $6,000 of personal savings with two partners. He carved out a successful niche for the company as a supplier of audio cards for computers. In 1992, Creative Technology became the first Singaporean company to be listed on the US Nasdaq exchange, and in 1994 it was listed on the main board in Singapore. In recent years, Creative Technology also started to focus on the internet.[5]

The pioneering pathway to affluence in Singapore today is certainly not dead. The concern is that the younger generation may become too risk-averse because of the availability of well-paying jobs and the small size of the domestic market. While hard data are not available, anecdotal evidence does suggest that some young Singapore entrepreneurs are seeking greener pastures elsewhere, especially in recent years in China and India. This may well be an unavoidable trend given Singapore's small domestic market size and hence relatively limited opportunities.

MARKET SIZE OF THE MASS AFFLUENT AND THE RICH

The size of the mass affluent households in Singapore is estimated at 62,500 in 2005, accounting for 5.9% of total households. By 2015, it is expected to increase to 117,200, or 9.1% of total households, a strong indicator of expanding prosperity. In 2005, their collective income was estimated at $8.7 billion. Assuming a conservative rate of real GDP growth of 4.5%, their total income is expected to reach $16.6 billion in 2015. Their average per household income, however, is not expected to change much between 2005 and 2015. Their discretionary spending is estimated at around 38% of their income.

Table 7.1

Size and Income of the Mass Affluent

Annual income $100,000 to $250,000 (2004 $ & exchange rate)	2005	2015	Cumulative annual growth
Number of Households	62,500	117,200	6.5%
Total Household Income	$8.7 billion	$16.6 billion	6.7%
Average Annual Household Income	$140,000	$141,400	0.1%
Per Household Discretionary Spending	$54,600	$55,100	0.9%

(MasterCard Asia/Pacific)

The rich households numbered 16,000 in 2005, or 1.5% of total households. It is expected to increase to 31,700 in 2015, accounting for 2.5% of total households. These households will have a collective income of over $12 billion in 2015, an impressive sum. Their average household income was estimated at just over $380,000 in 2005, and is not expected to change much in 2015. Their discretionary spending is impressively high. By 2015, it is estimated that on average each of the rich households will spend close to $150,000 on discretionary expenditures.

Table 7.2

Size and Income of the Rich

Annual income > $250,000 (constant 2004 $)	2005	2015	Cumulative annual growth
Number of Households	16,000	31,700	7.0%
Total Household Income	$6.1 billion	$12.1 billion	7.1%
Average Annual Household Income	$380,600	$383,300	0.1%
Per Household Discretionary Spending	$125,600	$149,500	1.8%

(MasterCard Asia/Pacific)

The biggest discretionary expenditure item of the mass affluent is "automobiles, PCs and mobile phones." Their spending on private healthcare, however, will be the fastest growing, along with spending on the "automobiles, PCs and mobile phones" category in the next 10 years. By 2015, the mass affluent households of Singapore will spend $3.5 billion on five key discretionary expenditure items as shown in Table 7.4.

Table 7.3

Key Discretionary Expenditure of the Mass Affluent

Key discretionary expenditure items (2004 $ billion)	2005	2015	Cumulative annual growth
Dining and Entertaining	0.7	1.0	3.6%
Shopping	0.5	0.8	4.8%
Travel & Leisure	0.2	0.3	4.6%
Private Health & Luxury Medicine	0.1	0.2	7.1%
Automobiles, PCs & Mobile Phones, etc.	0.6	1.2	7.1%
Total	2.1	3.5	5.2%

(MasterCard Asia/Pacific)

The rich households have a similar spending pattern as the mass affluent. Their spending on shopping, however, will be the fastest growing in the next decade. Together they will spend $2.7 billion in 2015 on the five key discretionary expenditure items.

Table 7.4

Key Discretionary Expenditure of the Rich

Key discretionary expenditure items (2004 $ billion)	2005	2015	Cumulative annual growth
Dining and Entertaining	0.5	0.8	4.8%
Shopping	0.3	0.7	8.8%
Travel & Leisure	0.1	0.2	7.1%
Private Health & Luxury Medicine	0.05	0.1	7.1%
Automobiles, PCs & Mobile Phones, etc.	0.5	0.9	6.1%
Total	1.5	2.7	6.1%

(MasterCard Asia/Pacific)

MALAYSIA

Malaysia has done well in spite of many apparent handicaps at the time of independence in 1967: an ethnically divided society and utter lack of modern industrial infrastructure, to name two. In 1969, it was rocked by racial riots between the Malay and the Chinese communities. In 1971, the government, led by then-Prime Minister Tun Razak, formulated the New Economic Plan (NEP), which aimed to address the disparity between the Malays and Chinese. It was a form of affirmative action, which reserved quotas for Malay students in universities and stipulated requirements for Malay ownership in any large corporations. Fortunately, the NEP was implemented with a "market friendly" approach, without sapping Malaysia's entrepreneurial energy, especially in the Chinese community. The net result was a gradual redistribution of the economic pie as the pie was growing bigger. Importantly, the Chinese community saw the size of their economic pie increase steadily even as their share of the total pie declined.

In the post-1997 years, many of the government's grandiose schemes, such as the "national car" project and the "multimedia super corridor" have proved to be counterproductive and unsustainable. Benefiting from the crisis, the Islamic opposition party, PAS, also made new gains in the northern states, a region known as the "Malay crescent" with predominantly rural and poor Malay communities.[6] The long-ruling, headstrong and frequently controversial Prime Minister Mohammad Mahathir stepped down in 2003, and his deputy Abdullah Ahmad Badawi took over. In 2004, Badawi won a landslide electoral victory and regained one of the two northern states held by PAS, providing him with a strong mandate both to govern and, as is widely expected, to reform the Malaysian economy and polity, especially in combating corruption and cronyism.

THE INHERITANCE PATHWAY TO AFFLUENCE

Like its neighbors, Malaysia has its share of large family-owned overseas Chinese businesses. The Yeoh family is a classic example. Yeoh Tiong Lay, the current patriarch of the family business YTL Corp., founded in 1955, controls one of Malaysia's largest conglomerates with interests in construction, utilities, hotels, property development and technology. Yeoh managed not only to survive the 1997 crisis, but actually benefited from it by buying up land and companies at bargain prices. In 2002, Yeoh moved abroad, buying the British utility company Wessex Water for $1.7 billion from the then-collapsing Enron. In 2005, YTL celebrated its 50th anniversary with VIP guests including Badawi. His son, Francis Yeoh, has run YTL Group since 1978, with the senior Yeoh remaining as executive chairman. With strong connections to the government, the group has been extraordinarily successful in winning government contracts to build bridges, highways and hospitals; and it built the express train linking the new airport to downtown Kuala Lumpur. A lifelong devotee of opera, Francis Yeoh counts Luciano Pavarotti as a close friend.

In the context of the NEP, however, there is another type of "inheritance" that has benefited entrepreneurial and politically connected Malays. Under the NEP, a Malay partner became mandatory by law for any sizable businesses, and this requirement opened up opportunities for politically well-connected Malays to move into the corporate sector on a fast track. If a Malay partner is required, then the Chinese business owner would certainly prefer one with strong political credentials and access to senior government officials. Thus, a whole generation of Malay entrepreneurs with good connections to the government got their head start in the corporate world. It should be said that many such Malay "partners" are content to be merely the figurehead of the business in return for financial reward. There are others, however, that used the opportunities to grow and expand.

Halim Saad, a former accountant with strong links to Malaysia's ruling United Malay National Organization (UMNO), for example, rose to take control of the Renong conglomerate. Tajudin Ramli, a well-connected former banker, came to national prominence when he took control of the national carrier Malaysian Airlines. He also controls Malaysia's largest mobile phone operator, Cellular Communications (Celcom). They were two leading names among a growing group of successful Malay business leaders (although both Saad and Ramli fell from grace in the post-crisis shakeout).

A more dramatic example of a fast track to the top is Syed Mokhtar Al Burkary, who started his working life as a humble rice trader. Today he controls, or has major stakes, in a mining company, airport, container port, auto manufacturing and other investments. *Forbes Asia* recently estimated his net worth at $1 billion.

THE PROFESSIONAL PATHWAY TO AFFLUENCE

With the introduction of the NEP, the civil service virtually became the turf of the Malays. Furthermore, with the quota system, more Malays have been able to graduate from universities, which in turn qualify them for positions within the government. This system has quickly created an urban Malay middle class; and for those rising to senior positions in government, they have also been able to join the ranks of the mass affluent. The expanding middle class itself, both Malay and non-Malay, generated new demands for well-paid professional services. For the well educated who qualify for such professional employment, it became the gateway to join the ranks of the mass affluent, and sometimes, the rich.

THE PIONEERING PATHWAY TO AFFLUENCE

As mentioned earlier, in spite of the NEP, Malaysia has remained a market conducive to encouraging and rewarding entrepreneurial efforts. The famous Robert Kuok is a self-made man who got started in agricultural commodity trading in the late 1940s after WWII; and then moved into shipping and real estate. Today, Kuok oversees a multinational business empire, the Kuok Group, which includes interests in air freight transport with landing rights in China and India; warehouse and cargo distribution centers in Hong Kong and China; sugar and oil plantations, mills and refinery in Southeast Asia; and Coca Cola bottling plants. It also operates the luxurious Shangri-La hotel chain, with 38 hotels throughout the Asia Pacific region.

Another legendary pioneering entrepreneur is Ananda Krishnan, who is from the Indian Tamil minority in Malaysia. Educated abroad, including at the Harvard Business School, he launched Malaysia's first satellite in 1996. His most impressive development is the massive Kuala Lumpur City Center, including the 88-story Petronas Twin Towers, which was briefly the world's tallest building.[7] In the same league as Krishnan is Vincent Tan, another self-made billionaire who built a business empire on gambling. His big break came when, in 1985, his Berjaya Group acquired the state-owned Sports Toto betting agency, no small tribute to his powerful political connections.

The pioneering pathway continues to function well in Malaysia, in spite of the ever-present ethnic politics. This result is largely due to impressive pragmatism shown by all the parties concerned: the government; the ethnically based political parties; the bureaucracy; and last but not least, the entrepreneurs themselves. In spite of often difficult circumstances, they have found ways to accommodate each other and have got on with the real business of making money.

MARKET SIZE OF THE MASS AFFLUENT AND THE RICH

Mass affluent households numbered 242,200 in 2005, which accounted for 4% of total households. They will increase to almost 560,000 in 2015, accounting for 7.3% of total households. In 2005, their collective annual income was $14.4 billion. Assuming a real GDP growth of 5.5% for the next 10 years, the total income of Malaysia's mass affluent households will reach $35.4 billion in 2015. Their average income, however, will only increase slightly in 2015 from their 2005 level. Their discretionary spending represents some 33% of their income, which is estimated at close to $21,000 in 2015.

Table 7.5
Size and Income of the Mass Affluent

Annual income $30,000 to $100,000 (2004 $ & exchange rate)	2005	2015	Cumulative annual growth
Number of Households	242,200	559,200	8.7%
Total Household Income	$14.4 billion	$35.4 billion	9.4%
Average Annual Household Income	$59,400	$63,300	0.6%
Per Household Discretionary Spending	$17,800	$20,900	1.6%

(MasterCard Asia/Pacific)

The rich households, on the other hand, numbered 34,450 in 2005, and will expand to 79,500 in 2015. They accounted for only 0.6% of total households in 2005, and are projected to account for some 1% of total households in 2015. Their collective income will grow fast, however, reaching $9.8 billion in 2015, up from $4 billion in 2005. Their discretionary spending will also reach $48,200 per household by 2015.

Table 7.6

Size and Income of the Rich

Annual income > $100,000 (constant 2004 $)	2005	2015	Cumulative annual growth
Number of Households	34,450	79,500	8.7%
Total Household Income	$4.0 billion	$9.8 billion	9.4%
Average Annual Household Income	$115,900	$123,500	0.6%
Per Household Discretionary Spending	$38,250	$48,200	2.3%

(MasterCard Asia/Pacific)

Dining and entertaining is the biggest of the five key discretionary expenditure items for Malaysia's mass affluent households. Spending on the "automobiles, PCs and mobile phones" category however, will be the fastest growing in the next 10 years. By 2015, spending on these five key items will top $7.8 billion.

Table 7.7
Key Discretionary Expenditure of the Mass Affluent

Key discretionary expenditure items (2004 $ billion)	2005	2015	Cumulative annual growth
Dining and Entertaining	1.7	3.5	7.5%
Shopping	0.4	0.9	8.7%
Travel & Leisure	0.3	0.7	9.5%
Private Health & Luxury Medicine	0.1	0.2	7.2%
Automobiles, PCs & Mobile Phones, etc.	0.9	2.5	10.6%
Total	3.4	7.8	8.7%

(MasterCard Asia/Pacific)

The overall pattern of spending by the rich households on the five key discretionary expenditure items is broadly similar. By 2015, they are expected to collectively spend $2.3 billion on these five key items.

Table 7.8
Key Discretionary Expenditure of the Rich

Key discretionary expenditure items (2004 $ billion)	2005	2015	Cumulative annual growth
Dining and Entertaining	0.5	1.0	7.2%
Shopping	0.1	0.3	8.7%
Travel & Leisure	0.1	0.2	7.1%
Private Health & Luxury Medicine	0.03	0.07	9.9%
Automobiles, PCs & Mobile Phones, etc.	0.3	0.7	10.6%
Total	1.0	2.3	8.7%

(MasterCard Asia/Pacific)

THAILAND

Thailand was at the epicenter of the 1997 crisis, which started with a massive devaluation of its currency, the baht. In the decade leading up to the crisis, Thailand was awash with foreign investment; and a long construction boom had led many Thais to joke that the crane (as in construction crane) had become the national bird of Thailand. Exploding private car ownership turned Bangkok into a round-the-clock traffic jam. To cope, many Thais had equipped their cars with modern versions of plastic chamber pots. And it was not uncommon at that time to find small portable refrigerators stocked with food and drinks inside the cars as well. So the Thais adapted to the circumstances and coped with an amazing and yet characteristic flexibility. And they did so again in coping with the aftermath of the crisis, until the economy made a successful recovery two years later.

The fact is the Thais had coped with many challenging circumstances and abrupt changes before. The absolute monarchy, which had skillfully avoided colonization by the Western powers in the 19th century, was forced in 1932 into becoming a constitutional monarchy by plotters in the military and the bureaucracy. And for 60 years afterward, the military dominated Thai politics. A series of military strongmen ruled until 1973, when student protests, which subsequently widened to involve the general public of Bangkok, brought down the military government. It was also the first time that the current king showed publicly and subtly his support for the students; he allowed the Royal Palace to be used to set up first-aid stations to care for students wounded in the protest.

In 1976, the military had again quietly resumed political control, and this time with the acquiescence of the general public, largely in reaction to the communist victories in Vietnam, Cambodia and Laos. In 1979, General Prem Tinsulanonda was appointed prime minister, and he introduced a form of "managed democracy," dubbed "Premocracy," which relied more on consensus building in the parliament and support from MPs from different parties and across the political spectrum. Prem had also built a reputation of being clean, and slowly gained the respect of the general public. The military tried twice to stage a coup against him, and failed both times when the king showed his support for Prem. He retired in 1988, succeeded by a civilian prime minister. Then, in 1991, another general, General Suchinda, staged a coup and took control. Opposition from the general public turned into bloodshed when Suchinda's forces fired into the crowd. The king again intervened, and Suchinda had to step down in disgrace.

Throughout this turbulent history, the Thai economy nevertheless managed to grow successfully. The Thais have several distinctive advantages. The first is clearly the institution of the monarchy personified by the current king, who in his long reign has gained the respect and devotion of the vast majority of his subjects. It in turn symbolizes the strong sense of social cohesion felt by the Thais, summed up in their nationalist prescript of "Nation; Religion (Buddhism), and King." Thus, in spite of turbulent politics, the Thais enjoy a sense of social cohesion that is akin to the ballast of a ship that keeps it from capsizing in a storm.[8]

Closely related to the first is its history of successful integration of Chinese immigrants in the Thai society, unique in Southeast Asia. Indeed, the king himself acknowledges some Chinese ancestry. The entrepreneurial skills and connections of these immigrants, who took Thai names and adopted Thai cultural practices remarkably well (in many instances facilitated by a shared Buddhist tradition), have proved to be a boon to the expansion and development of Thai commerce domestically as well as in the region, and indeed globally.

Finally, the Thais are among the best educated in the region, especially the women. In fact, in recent years women are better represented than men in tertiary education in professional schools such as law, business and medicine. These better educated generations, men and women, in the context of rapid urbanization, form the core of an increasingly sophisticated consumer class in Thailand, driving the growth of a vibrant consumer market.

THE INHERITANCE PATHWAY TO AFFLUENCE

The most prominent among leading Thai family businesses is the Charoen Pokphand Group (the CP Group). Charoen Pokphand means "commodity development" in Thai, which reflects precisely the historical origin of the business. It was started in 1921 by two brothers, Chinese immigrants from Shantou, the home county of the Teochiu dialect group (thus of the same ethnic background as Hong Kong's Li Ka-shing). They set up a vegetable seeds operation in Bangkok, and later expanded into supplying farmers with fertilizer and plant pesticides. They leveraged their Chinese connections to expand the business, importing seeds from China and exporting poultry, eggs and other agricultural products back to China. The business grew and, following the overseas Chinese networks, they established outlets in Hong Kong, Singapore, Kuala Lumpur and Taipei.

Dhanin Chearavanont was born to one of the two brothers in Bangkok in 1939, the youngest of four sons. He attended high school in China and college in Hong Kong, and joined the family business back in Bangkok in the 1960s. Shortly thereafter, he introduced a radical innovation, contract farming, which fundamentally transformed the business and propelled the CP Group into the top league of business in Thailand. Working with Bangkok Bank, founded by another Chinese immigrant, Chin Sophonpanich, Dhanin could extend credit to farmers to allow them to buy seeds, fertilizer and pesticides. He then guaranteed to buy their produce back at pre-agreed prices. Thus the CP Group became both seller and buyer to the farmers, while enabling them to reduce risks and to produce at a scale not feasible without the CP Group. Dhanin later applied the same approach to working with farmers to develop chicken and shrimp farming. Within a decade, CP Group became the largest agribusiness in Southeast Asia.

Dhanin became group president in 1979. With the opening of China, he expanded rapidly into the China market in the 1980s and 1990s. Within a decade, CP Group had 70 feed mills covering

30 of the 31 provinces of China (except Tibet). As the China market expanded, so did CP Group's business. Dhanin formed partnerships in China with Honda in motorcycles, Heineken in beer production and Siemens in electronics. Dhanin, now in his 60s and an enthusiast in raising homing pigeons, is the quintessential Thai-Chinese businessman. He has built excellent relationships with the top leaders in China and is an advisor to the Chinese government, while at home he is a strong supporter of the king and maintains close relations with virtually all the Thai administrations. He is a true captain of Thai industry.[9]

Dhanin represents the tip of a very large iceberg in inherited wealth in Thailand. Other instances of family wealth are, of course, several orders of magnitude smaller, but like Dhanin's, much of it is of Chinese immigrant origin. Many of these families are passing the inheritance to a new and well-educated generation, who are ready to reinvent their parents' traditional businesses. Thus, in many cases, the inheritance pathway to affluence is feeding into the pioneering pathway to affluence in an inter-generational context in Thailand.

THE PROFESSIONAL PATHWAY TO AFFLUENCE

As exemplified by the CP Group, more Thai businesses today are going global (or at least operating within the Southeast Asia region), in spite of their traditional family-run background. This process entails professionalizing the management, which creates better-paid employment, and thus contribute to the professional pathway to affluence. An expanding middle class also generates higher demand for professional services such as in personal finance, the legal sector, accounting and in private healthcare, especially in urban areas. Again, many jobs created in these areas are highly paid, qualifying the job holders to join the ranks of the mass affluent, if not always the rich. The professional pathway to affluence in Thailand is set to become more important in the coming years for the well educated and highly skilled Thai professionals.

THE PIONEERING PATHWAY TO AFFLUENCE

In spite of rapid changes, Thailand has remained a market where pioneering entrepreneurs have been able to flourish. Among the leading businesses of Thailand are many self-made successes. Take Charoen Sirivadhanabhakdi, for example. Charoen is known as the Whiskey King of Thailand, and his Thai Beverage empire has long been the market leader in Thailand for hard liquor, including the famous Mekong whiskey. He built his business up from scratch, starting out with just his personal savings in his pocket. Another famous self-made business success is Anant Asavabhokin. His company, Land & Houses, is Thailand's largest builder of affordable housing. He capitalized early on Thailand's urbanization and built affordable homes for the burgeoning middle class. He also introduced innovative ideas from abroad, such as his do-it-yourself hardware and home furnishing business, HomePro.

A more controversial example is Thaksin Shinawatra, the deposed prime minister of Thailand. A self-made billionaire, his company, Shin Corp., began by selling and leasing IBM mainframe computers in 1983. Seven years later Shin went public on the Bangkok Stock Exchange, and became Thailand's leading telecom group. He stepped down from running the business directly in 1994 to assume the post of minister of foreign affairs. He launched his bid for prime minister by establishing the Thai Rak Thai Party, which became Thailand's ruling party. Throughout his business and political career, however, there have been accusations of corruption and unethical practices. The way he managed to sell Shin Corp. to Temasek Holdings, a Singapore government-linked investment firm, in a multibillion dollar transaction, without having to pay any tax, was one of the catalysts that plunged Thailand into a political crisis in 2006, and Thaksin was subsequently deposed in a military coup.

Entrepreneurship has always flourished in Thailand, and will continue to do so in the coming years. The pioneering pathway to affluence is in good working order and will deliver many Thais to the ranks of the mass affluent and rich in the next decade.

MARKET SIZE OF THE MASS AFFLUENT AND THE RICH

The size of the mass affluent was estimated at 160,300 households in 2005, accounting for only 0.9% of total households. By 2015, it is expected that their number will increase to almost 400,000 households, or some 1.9% of total households. Assuming a growth rate of 5.8% per year in the next 10 years, their collective income will reach over $21 billion in 2015, up from $8.5 billion in 2005. At around $53,000, their household income is not expected to change much, however. About one-third of their annual income is spent on discretionary expenditures, which is estimated at $17,600 in 2015.

Table 7.9
Size and Income of the Mass Affluent

Annual income $30,000 to $100,000 (2004 $ & exchange rate)	2005	2015	Cumulative annual growth
Number of Households	160,300	395,800	9.4%
Total Household Income	$8.5 billion	$21.1 billion	9.6%
Average Annual Household Income	$52,700	$53,400	0.1%
Per Household Discretionary Spending	$15,800	$17,600	1.1%

(MasterCard Asia/Pacific)

Rich households numbered 19,700 in 2005, and will increase to 48,500 in 2015. They account for only a small percentage of total households, however: 0.1% in 2005, and 0.2% in 2015. Collectively their income will grow quite fast, rising to $6.1 billion in 2015, up from $2.5 billion in 2005. Their average household income is also impressive, estimated at $124,700 in 2005 and increasing marginally to $126,300 in 2015. Their discretionary spending, however, will rise faster, from just over $40,000 per household in 2005, to around $50,000 in 2015.

Table 7.10

Size and Income of the Rich

Annual income > $100,000 (constant 2004 $)	2005	2015	Cumulative annual growth
Number of Households	19,700	48,500	9.4%
Total Household Income	$2.5 billion	$6.1 billion	9.3%
Average Annual Household Income	$124,700	$126,300	0.1%
Per Household Discretionary Spending	$41,150	$49,260	1.8%

(MasterCard Asia/Pacific)

Dining and entertaining is the biggest discretionary expenditure item among the mass affluent, but spending on automobiles and PCs, etc., will be the fastest growing in the next decade. By 2015, the mass affluent will spend $5.3 billion on the five key discretionary expenditure items.

Table 7.11

Key Discretionary Expenditure of the Mass Affluent

Key discretionary expenditure items (2004 $ billion)	2005	2015	Cumulative annual growth
Dining and Entertaining	$1.1	$2.3	7.5%
Shopping	$0.3	$0.7	9.9%
Travel & Leisure	$0.1	$0.4	10.6%
Private Health & Luxury Medicine	$0.07	$0.2	10.5%
Automobiles, PCs & Mobile Phones, etc.	$0.6	$1.7	11.5%
Total	$2.2	$5.3	9.3%

(MasterCard Asia/Pacific)

While sharing a similar overall spending pattern as the mass affluent, the rich households' fastest growing discretionary expenditure item is private health and luxury medicine. Some $1.6 billion will be spent by the rich households on the five discretionary expenditure items in 2015.

Table 7.12

Key Discretionary Expenditure of the Rich

Key discretionary expenditure items (2004 $ billion)	2005	2015	Cumulative annual growth
Dining and Entertaining	$0.3	$0.7	7.6%
Shopping	$0.07	$0.2	10.0%
Travel & Leisure	$0.04	$0.1	10.2%
Private Health & Luxury Medicine	$0.02	$0.07	13.3%
Automobiles, PCs & Mobile Phones, etc.	$0.2	$0.5	9.6%
Total	$0.6	$1.6	10.3%

(MasterCard Asia/Pacific)

INDONESIA

Indonesia was without question the worst affected among all the crisis-hit Southeast Asian countries in 1997. The government of the long-ruling strongman, Suharto, fell in its aftermath. A succession of ineffective presidents followed, and it was not until Susilo Bambang Yudhoyono, a former general, became president through Indonesia's first direct presidential election in 2004, that serious attempts were made to reform the economy and revive economic growth.

Suharto, a general himself, took power in 1965, after a communist-inspired rising against the founding president Sukarno failed. Massive bloodshed ensued. Backed by the military, Suharto took control and installed an authoritarian government with himself as president. He also introduced a new economic development program, known as the "New Order." The New Order succeeded spectacularly between 1965 and 1997; with inflation brought under control, economic infrastructure improved, the manufacturing sector grew, and the agricultural sector revived. For example, in 1983, Indonesia produced its first rice surplus in 100 years, thanks to the government's investment in improving rural infrastructure.[10] With rich endowment in natural resources and rising investment, oil, gas and mining outputs also rose rapidly. For over three decades, Suharto's authoritarian rule delivered the goods of economic growth to most Indonesians, with an embryonic middle class gradually taking shape.

Three decades of authoritarian rule, however, also created many deep structural problems that were being embedded in the system. Business development was dominated by the Suharto family and a clique of cronies. Favoritism in granting business licenses, government contracts and bank loans was the means for Suharto to control how business was done and by whom. Favoritism started out as a reward to his cronies and close supporters and (to the distaste of the vast majority of Indonesians) his own children; then it became the norm and eventually turned into abusive excess. It also brought with it all the problems of resource misallocation and economic inefficiency such that it steadily eroded the productivity of the Indonesian economy.

When the 1997 crisis arrived, the Indonesian economy was already bedeviled with structural problems of all kinds. Grandiose projects to produce a national car (inspired by the ill-considered Malaysian example of Proton) and the development of an aerospace industry had all floundered. More critically the fruits of growth had stopped flowing to the masses but were captured by an ever-smaller group of Suharto cronies instead. The 1997 crisis wiped out a great deal of the ill-gotten fortunes of the Suharto cronies, but it also saddled the average Indonesian with a stagnant economy, unemployment, high inflation, lack of foreign investment and slow or no growth in personal income. These are problems that President Yudhoyono and his team of reform-minded technocrats have been attempting to solve ever since they came to power in 2004.

THE INHERITANCE PATHWAY TO AFFLUENCE

A sordid story of how the inheritance pathway to affluence functioned under Suharto involved his own family. His four children, arrogant and ambitious, all built their own billion-dollar business empires in property, banking, telecom, media and transport. It was a perverse conversion of political inheritance (being children of the ruling strongman) into business inheritance. It worked as follows: the children started their own companies, more or less on paper and nothing else. Coveted licenses and government contracts were then handed out to them by government ministries and agencies. With these licenses and contracts in hand, the Suharto children had no problem signing up eager investors and business partners, who brought the needed capital and management expertise. Knowing that there would not be any competition for such licenses, and with government contracts in hand, the Suharto children and their business partners then fixed prices to maximize profits. By the mid-1990s, Suharto's four children, plus his daughter-in-law, one cousin and one half brother, represented possibly the biggest concentration of wealth in a single family in Asia.

Ever since the fall of Suharto, the various governments have been trying to untangle and unearth the dirty dealings of the Suharto clan. Suharto's son, Tommy, was formally charged with corruption in court in 1999. The clan still has massive wealth in Indonesia and very likely stashed overseas as well. Many currently active top officials and businessmen had been partners of the Suharto clan in their corrupt dealings and therefore they all have incentives to hush things up. Furthermore, the judicial system being what it is in Indonesia, it is likely that it will be a long time before all the details are known and all the culprits brought to justice.

Apart from the Suharto legacy, however, Indonesia does have legitimate inherited wealth, and, not surprisingly, a great deal of it is controlled by the Indonesian-Chinese. The most famous of the Indonesian-Chinese family business is today run by Anthoni Liem, son of billionaire Liem Sioe Liong. The flagship of their business empire is Indofood, the largest food producer in the country. The Liem family originally came from southern China and belongs to the same Teochiu dialect group (hence the same as Thailand's Dhanin and Hong Kong's Li Ka-shing). The family business, like many other overseas Chinese businesses, started out in trading. Then the Liems quickly moved into timbers and mining, agribusiness, and banking and finance. Liem himself cultivated a close friendship with Suharto, which, not surprisingly, came back to haunt him after the fall of Suharto. During the anti-Chinese riots in 1999, an angry mob destroyed his home in Jakarta. The family business has, however, survived and continued to prosper. It is the same with many other large Indonesian-Chinese family businesses. They have adapted to the new environment and adjusted their business practice accordingly, just as they had done so many times in the past.

THE PROFESSIONAL PATHWAY TO AFFLUENCE

It is not an exaggeration to say that the 1997 crisis shut down Indonesia's professional pathway to affluence. In order for this pathway to work, as demonstrated in other markets, well-paid professional employment has to grow, typically driven by strong foreign direct investment and an expanding middle class. Neither has happened in recent years in Indonesia. Investment prospects (both foreign and domestic) have been improving since President Yudhoyono's election, but it will be at least a few more years before the growth of professional employment picks up significantly. Until this happens, the professional pathway to affluence in Indonesia remains hugely under-utilized.

THE PIONEERING PATHWAY TO AFFLUENCE

Apart from the well-known success of the Indonesian-Chinese business community, there is actually quite a sizeable group of pioneering and successful entrepreneurs who are indigenous Indonesians (or more accurately Javanese). Interestingly, many of the leading Javanese businessmen made their initial fortunes in manufacturing and selling clove cigarettes. These cigarettes are unique to Indonesia, made with tobacco mixed with clove, high in tar and nicotine content, and with a particularly pungent taste. They are one of the few indulgences affordable to the masses of working class Indonesians. So the market for clove cigarettes is a huge one in Indonesia; and demand has proved to be stable even in times of severe economic downturn as in the immediate post-1997 years. Working-class Indonesians would cut back on food consumption first before they cut back on clove cigarettes.

In 2005, Rachman Halim's clove cigarette manufacturer, PT Gudang Garam, ranked number one in market share in Indonesia. He was followed by Putera Sampoerna, and by Budi Hartono, whose company, Djarum, had the third largest market share.[11] They are all self-made successful entrepreneurs (albeit Halim is the scion of the founding Wonowidjojo clan). Some are also moving into new business ventures. Sampoerna, for example, recently sold his company to Philip Morris and has gone into developing luxury casinos. Hartono has also diversified into banking and property development.

As its economy recovers, Indonesia will likely prove to be a hotbed for pioneering entrepreneurs in the coming years. An expanding middle class, while critical for the professional pathway to affluence to work, is also vital for creating new business opportunities for the pioneering entrepreneurs. Large urban centers like Jakarta will be especially important for this development.

MARKET SIZE OF THE MASS AFFLUENT
AND THE RICH

The mass affluent households numbered 382,200 in 2005, and are expected to grow quite fast to 786,300 by 2015. In 2005, they accounted for only 0.7% of total households; and by 2015, a forecasted 1.1%. Their total income in 2005 was estimated at $10 billion. Assuming a trend rate of real GDP growth of 5.5% in the next 10 years, their collective household income will rise to over $21 billion. On a per household basis, their annual income will rise from $25,600 in 2005, to $27,100 in 2015. Their discretionary spending per household is expected to grow only very marginally from about $7,700 in 2005, to just over $8,000 in 2015.

Table 7.13

Size and Income of the Mass Affluent

Annual income $15,000 to $75,000 (2004 $ & exchange rate)	2005	2015	Cumulative annual growth
Number of Households	382,200	786,300	7.5%
Total Household Income	$10.0 billion	$21.1 billion	7.8%
Average Annual Household Income	$25,600	$27,100	5.7%
Per Household Discretionary Spending	$7,680	$8,100	0.5%

(MasterCard Asia/Pacific)

The number of rich households in 2005 was estimated at 80,000, accounting for only 0.15% of total households. By 2015, this segment is expected to increase to 120,000, or 0.16% of total households. Their estimated average household income, however, was a remarkable $87,000 in 2005; and it should be $101,000 in 2015. Their discretionary spending on average is about 39% of their annual income, yielding an impressive $39,400 per household in 2015.

Table 7.14

Size and Income of the Rich

Annual income > $75,000 (constant 2004 $)	2005	2015	Cumulative annual growth
Number of Households	80,000	120,000	4.1%
Total Household Income	$6.9 billion	$12.1 billion	5.8%
Average Annual Household Income	$87,000	$101,000	1.5%
Per Household Discretionary Spending	$28,700	$39,400	3.2%

(MasterCard Asia/Pacific)

Due to limited data availability, the breakdown of the discretionary spending by expenditure items in Indonesia is not as detailed as in other markets. Only four key expenditure items can be identified: dining and entertaining; shopping and automobiles; travel and related leisure activities; and private health and luxury medicine. Of the four, spending on dining and entertaining is the biggest item for the mass affluent, but spending on private healthcare is expected to be the fastest growing. By 2015, the mass affluent is projected to spend over $5 billion on these four key expenditures.

Table 7.15

Key Discretionary Expenditure of the Mass Affluent

Key discretionary expenditure items (2004 $ billion)	2005	2015	Cumulative annual growth
Dining and Entertaining	$1.7	$2.9	5.5%
Shopping & Automobiles	$0.8	$1.5	6.5%
Travel & Leisure	$0.1	$0.3	11.6%
Private Health & Luxury Medicine	$0.1	$0.4	14.8%
Total	$2.7	$5.1	6.6%

(MasterCard Asia/Pacific)

The rich households share a similar spending pattern as the mass affluent, with dining and entertaining being the biggest spending item. For the rich households, however, spending on travel and related leisure activities will be the fastest growing. It is estimated that some $4.4 billion will be spent by the rich households on the four key expenditure items in 2015.

Table 7.16

Key Discretionary Expenditure of the Rich

Key discretionary expenditure items (2004 $ billion)	2005	2015	Cumulative annual growth
Dining and Entertaining	$0.9	$1.8	7.2%
Shopping & Automobiles	$0.7	$1.4	7.1%
Travel & Leisure	$0.3	$0.9	11.6%
Private Health & Luxury Medicine	$0.2	$0.5	9.6%
Total	$2.1	$4.4	7.7%

(MasterCard Asia/Pacific)

THE PHILIPPINES

In the early years after WWII, the Philippines' development prospects were better than virtually every other market in Asia. It had large quantities of US foreign aid, a highly educated population conversant in English and abundant natural resources. In the 1960s, only Japan had a standard of living higher than the Philippines. But instead of becoming one of the East Asian tigers, per capita GDP in the Philippines declined by 7.2% between 1980 and 1992.[12]

Much of the blame can be placed on the Marcos regime. Ferdinand Marcos, who ruled as a dictator after declaring martial law in 1972, was justifiably blamed for rampant corruption and creating an oligarchy based on collusions between large businesses, Marcos own clan and cronies, and the military. Marcos was ousted in 1986, and Corazon Aquino, widow of the assassinated (widely believed to be Marcos' handiwork) opposition leader Benigno Aquino, became president and restored democracy. The economy, however, failed to revive; and it was not until Fidel Ramos, a former general, was elected president in 1992 that serious efforts in reforming the economy started.

Growth picked up to the 5-7% range per year by the mid-1990s. But then it ran out of steam. With hindsight, it is clear that the Ramos administration had been successful only in completing the easier reform tasks, but failed to tackle the entrenched constraints on the economy. The Ramos government, for example, had been able to remove arbitrary import restrictions, but did not have the capacity to raise higher value-added exports; and while it could dismantle some of the perverse fiscal incentives, it failed to create a revenue system capable of supporting long-term investments in badly needed infrastructure.[13] As a consequence, the economy remains stuck with crumbling public infrastructure, a precarious government fiscal position, chronic high unemployment and recurring bouts of macroeconomic instability. All this has been made worse by a persistently volatile political environment. Political infighting between powerful factions periodically turned into public confrontations in recent years, as in the ousting of former President Joseph Estrada, and several attempts at ousting his successor Gloria Arroyo.

Frustrated with the lack of opportunities at home, Filipinos have gone overseas in search of work in increasing numbers. Today, between eight million and nine million Filipinos work overseas; their remittances back to the Philippines have become a financial lifeline for many low- to middle-income Philippine families. Total remittances have amounted to around 10% of GDP in recent years.

THE INHERITANCE PATHWAY TO AFFLUENCE

Arguably this is the most important pathway to affluence in the Philippines. Two groups of "old money" dominate. The Filipino-Spanish old money known as the *illustrados*, which includes the Ayala, Lopez, Cojuangco and Soriano clans; and the Filipino-Chinese old money that includes names like John Gokongwei, Henry Sy and Lucio Tan.

The Ayala clan, for example, is about 170 years old with business interests in real estate, banking, hotels, agribusiness, financial services, electronics, aviation and telecom. In other words, it is a true conglomerate. In 1995, the management was passed down to the Harvard-educated Jaime Augusto Zobel de Ayala II, then age 36, in a smooth transition. The flagship of the group is Ayala Land, which developed the famous Ayala Triangle in the glamorous downtown financial district of Makati in Manila.

Among the Filipino-Chinese old money, John Gokongwei is perhaps the most famous. Born in Cebu but able to trace his ancestry to Fujian province in China (hence belonging to the Hokkien dialect group), he inherited the family business and drove it in a massive expansion over a 20-year period. He took advantage of the bear market in the immediate aftermath of the fall of Marcos and bought up prime real estate at bargain prices in the now premium Ortigas business district in Manila. He built his flagship Robinson's Galleria Mall there, and it draws over 50 million visitors a year today. His vast business interests span property development, retail, telecom, power supply, petroleum and minerals.

Changes in the political arena rarely affect the fortunes of these large family-owned businesses. With experience and ample practice, they are all experts in adapting to changing political conditions. They seem to know when to batten down the hatches and stay low, and when to surface to throw their weight behind certain politicians on their way up. In any event, the leading business families and leading political families are intertwined at an astonishing degree through marriages, shared backgrounds and business dealings. Together, they take good care of themselves and of each other.

THE PROFESSIONAL PATHWAY TO AFFLUENCE

The professional pathway to affluence in the Philippines cannot be said to be functioning well. This is largely due to limited opportunities in well-paid professional employment within the country. A direct consequence of this is the large and rising outflow of Philippines' human resource in seeking work overseas. Sadly, many of these overseas workers are university educated but employed in jobs abroad at far below their professional capacity. Their remittances, however, have become important not only for their own family members in the Philippines, but increasingly for stabilizing the Philippines' balance of payment as well. While making a significant contribution to the Philippine economy, these overseas workers are not making progress on their own pathway to affluence.

THE PIONEERING PATHWAY TO AFFLUENCE

With the right political connections, pioneering entrepreneurs could make it big now and again in the Philippines. William Gatchalian, for example, did well through his close relationship with former President Estrada. A Filipino-Chinese from Fujian province, he first went into real estate development, capitalizing on the rising overseas remittances received by lower income families who aspired to own their own home. He made his initial break by developing low-cost housing in the province of Cavite, Bulacan and Cebu, targeting precisely the families that benefited from overseas remittances. He went into central Manila only much later after developing powerful political and business connections. His business interests then expanded, and he was a pioneer in launching the domestic carrier Air Philippines in 1995, challenging Lucio Tan, arguably Philippines' leading business bigwig, who controls the large but poorly-run Philippine Airlines. With more than a touch of irony, Estrada made Gatchalian, someone who knew how to grow rich from the overseas workers, the government's advisor on overseas workers affairs.

The example of Gatchalian notwithstanding, the Philippines is not exactly a hotbed of entrepreneurial start-ups and successes. Entrepreneurs without any political and business connections face formidable challenges. To begin with, bureaucratic obstruction and red tape could sink many a good business idea. As convincingly documented by Hernando de Soto, the Philippines is among one of the most difficult places in the world to set up a new small business.[14] On the positive side, there is clearly no shortage of talent and skills and risk-taking appetite, evidenced by the growing army of overseas workers. If and when the domestic environment improves, this huge reservoir of talent in the Philippines could easily turn the pioneering pathway to affluence into a highway to riches.

MARKET SIZE OF THE MASS AFFLUENT AND THE RICH

The mass affluent numbered 291,600 households in 2005, accounting for 1.7% of total households, and is expected to increase to 565,300 households in 2015, or 2.7% of total households. Collectively they had almost $11 billion of income in 2005. Assuming a trend rate of real GDP growth of 5%, their income is estimated to rise to just over $20 billion in 2015. Their average household income, however, is expected to drop from $37,380 in 2005, to $35,600 in 2015. This is largely due to the fact that more households are expected to join the ranks of the mass affluent over the next 10 years with annual income below the 2005 average. So the average household income of the mass affluent will decrease by about 0.05% per year. Their discretionary spending, estimated at about 33% of income, will also decrease at a similar pace.

Table 7.17

Size and Income of the Mass Affluent

Annual income $15,000 to $75,000 (2004 $ & exchange rate)	2005	2015	Cumulative annual growth
Number of Households	291,600	565,300	6.8%
Total Household Income	$10.9 billion	$20.1 billion	6.3%
Average Annual Household Income	$37,380	$35,600	-0.05%
Per Household Discretionary Spending	$12,300	$11,700	-0.06%

(MasterCard Asia/Pacific)

The size of the rich households is much smaller. In 2005 it numbered only 14,800, and is expected to increase to 28,600 by 2015. In 2005, it accounted for a minuscule 0.08% of total households, and by 2015, it should be only 0.14% of total households. Their average income is, however, high. In 2005, it was estimated at almost $90,000, and is projected to rise to over $90,000 by 2015. Their average discretionary spending will increase a bit faster, reaching $35,300 per household in 2015, up from just under $30,000 in 2005.

Table 7.18

Size and Income of the Rich

Annual income > $75,000 (constant 2004 $)	2005	2015	Cumulative annual growth
Number of Households	14,800	28,600	6.8%
Total Household Income	$1.3 billion	$2.5 billion	6.7%
Average Annual Household Income	$89,400	$90,500	0.1%
Per Household Discretionary Spending	$29,500	$35,300	2.1%

(MasterCard Asia/Pacific)

The mass affluent spend most on dining and entertaining, but their spending on the "automobiles, PCs and mobile phones" category will be the fastest growing. Together, they will spend about $5.4 billion in 2015 on the five key discretionary expenditure items.

Table 7.19

Key Discretionary Expenditure of the Mass Affluent

Key discretionary expenditure items (2004 $ billion)	2005	2015	Cumulative annual growth
Dining and Entertaining	$2.0	$3.2	4.9%
Shopping	$0.6	$1.2	6.8%
Travel & Leisure	$0.04	$0.1	7.4%
Private Health & Luxury Medicine	$0.1	$0.2	7.2%
Automobiles, PCs & Mobile Phones, etc.	$0.3	$0.7	8.8%
Total	$3.1	$5.4	5.8%

(MasterCard Asia/Pacific)

The rich households have a similar spending pattern as the mass affluent, with dining and entertaining being the biggest spending item. But their spending on travel and related leisure activities will be the fastest growing. By 2015, the 28,600 rich households in the Philippines will spend $700 million on the five discretionary expenditure items as shown in Table 7.20.

Table 7.20

Key Discretionary Expenditure of the Rich

Key discretionary expenditure items (2004 $ billion)	2005	2015	Cumulative annual growth
Dining and Entertaining	$0.2	$0.4	4.9%
Shopping	$0.07	$0.14	7.2%
Travel & Leisure	$0.01	$0.03	11.6%
Private Health & Luxury Medicine	$0.01	$0.02	7.1%
Automobiles, PCs & Mobile Phones, etc.	$0.08	$0.14	5.8%
Total	$0.4	$0.7	5.8%

(MasterCard Asia/Pacific)

In summary, the mass affluent and the rich households in Southeast Asia command very impressive purchasing power. Forecasts of their discretionary spending are summarized in Table 7.21. Malaysia has the highest combined discretionary spending by the mass affluent and rich, estimated at $15.5 billion in 2015. Tiny Singapore shares the second place with Indonesia. Thailand comes third, followed by the Philippines. Together, the projected discretionary spending by the mass affluent and rich in Southeast Asia amounts to almost $55 billion in 2015.

Table 7.21

Discretionary Spending in 2015

	Mass affluent	Rich	Total
Indonesia	$6.5 billion	$4.7 billion	$11.2 billion
Malaysia	$11.7 billion	$3.8 billion	$15.5 billion
Philippines	$6.6 billion	$1.0 billion	$7.6 Billion
Singapore	$6.5 billion	$4.7 billion	$11.2 billion
Thailand	$6.9 billion	$2.4 billion	$9.3 billion
Total of five markets			$54.8 billion

(MasterCard Worldwide, Asia/Pacific)

As described in this chapter, the ways in which the three pathways to affluence function are very different between these five Southeast Asian markets. Such differences are reflected in their respective consumption patterns, value perceptions and priorities. For example, those with "old money," be they of Spanish or Chinese origins, are more discreet and less flamboyant as a rule. Successful Chinese business entrepreneurs in Indonesia and the Philippines also have additional reasons to be discreet regardless of the vintage of their money-not to provoke the envy and unwanted attention of the locals.

Rapidly expanding professional employment in Singapore, Malaysia and Thailand is shifting the professional pathway to affluence into a higher gear. This in turn is creating a bigger mass affluent market, dominated by well-educated, and therefore more technologically savvy and sophisticated, consumers. Even though many of these consumers are becoming affluent for the first time, their behavior is unlikely to be the same as that of the stereotypical nouveau riche. Make no mistake, however, there will be a lot of nouveaux riches in Southeast Asia in the next 10 years. Like *nouveaux riches* elsewhere, they will be loud and they will be conspicuous. And they will want attention.

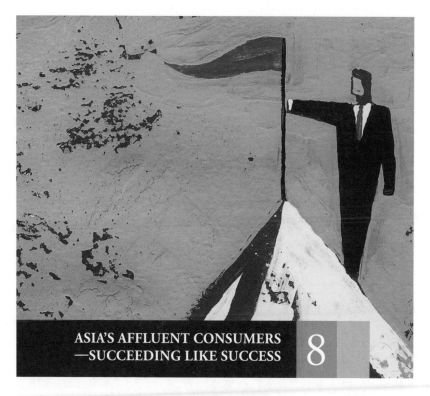

ASIA'S AFFLUENT CONSUMERS —SUCCEEDING LIKE SUCCESS $\quad 8$

As documented in previous chapters, the size and spending power of the affluent and rich consumers of Asia are expected to expand quickly in the coming years to 2015. The amount of purchasing power that they will command is nothing less than astonishing. For the mass affluent households in the 12 Asian markets examined, their estimated discretionary spending by 2015 will reach almost half a trillion dollars. For the rich households, it will reach almost $110 billion. Combined, their spending power will be about $610 billion dollars.

First let's take a deeper look at the affluent households' spending in Chart 8.1. The horizontal axis of the chart represents the per capita income of the markets estimated for 2015, using their respective trend rates of real GDP growth cited in earlier chapters.[1] The vertical axis represents the size of the mass affluent households (in log scale to create a more readable format). Thus, in one glance, the discretionary spending power of each of the markets is represented by the size of their circles, and their locations indicate the size of their mass affluent and the overall per capita income of the market.

The size of the circles represents the amount of discretionary spending estimated for 2015. Japan, with the biggest circle, is located in the upper right corner of the chart because it has the highest per capita income and its size of the mass affluent households is also among one of the biggest in the region. The circle representing China, on the other hand, is found in the upper left corner of the chart. This is because its per capita income is among the lowest in the region, but it has the highest number of mass affluent households. And the size of China's circle, representing the total discretionary spending of its mass affluent in 2015, is second only to that of Japan. Data details for each of the markets are summarized in Table 8.1 (the countries are ranked in the table in their order of appearance in the book).

Chart 8.1

Discretionary Spending of "Mass Affluent" Households in 2015

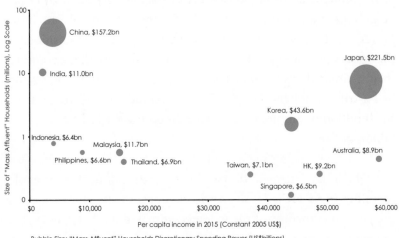

Bubble Size: "Mass Affluent" Households Discretionary Spending Power (US$billions)

Table 8.1

Size & Discretionary Spending of Mass Affluent Households in 2015

	Discretionary Spending	Number of Households
Japan	$221.5 billion	7.1 million
China	$157.2 billion	44.9 million
India	$11.0 billion	10.5 million
Australia	$8.9 billion	425,000
Korea	$43.6 billion	1.5 million
Taiwan	$7.1 billion	253,700
Hong Kong	$9.2 billion	251,700
Singapore	$6.5 billion	117,200
Malaysia	$11.7 billion	559,200
Thailand	$6.9 billion	395,800
Indonesia	$6.4 billion	786,300
Philippines	$6.6 billion	565,300
Total	**$496.6 billion**	**67.4 million**

Now let's look at the total discretionary spending power of the rich households of the 12 key Asian markets. By 2015, it is estimated that it will reach over $108 billion. The market-specific discretionary spending power of the rich households is illustrated in Chart 8.2, structured in the same format as Chart 8.1. In Chart 8.2, most of the circles representing the 12 markets are very different in size and location from Chart 8.1. While Japan more or less occupies the same position and is the biggest in size, Korea is in second place in terms of size. China moved from the upper left corner down to a position in the middle left, with a smaller circle, reflecting both the fewer number of rich households and their smaller total discretionary spending power. Data details of the rich households are summarized in Table 8.2 (again, countries ranked in accordance with appearance in the book).

Chart 8.2

Discretionary Spending of "Rich" Households in 2015

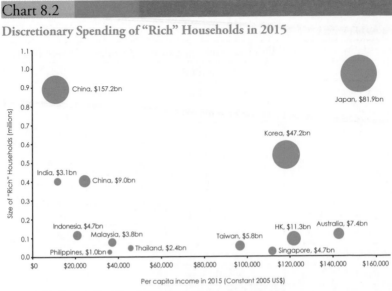

Per capita income in 2015 (Constant 2005 US$)

Bubble Size: "Mass Affluent" Households Discretionary Spending Power (US$billions)

Table 8.2

Size & Discretionary Spending of Rich Households in 2015

	Discretionary Spending	**Number of Households**
Japan	$8.2 billion	967,000
China	$9.0 billion	405,200
India	$3.1 billion	405,500
Australia	$7.4 billion	118,850
Korea	$47.2 billion	542,000
Taiwan	$5.8 billion	59,500
Hong Kong	$11.3 billion	94,250
Singapore	$4.7 billion	31,700
Malaysia	$3.8 billion	79,500
Thailand	$2.4 billion	48,500
Indonesia	$4.7 billion	120,000
Philippines	$1.0 billion	28,600
Total	**$108.6 billion**	**2.8 million**

Given their impressive purchasing power, what are the mass affluent and the rich like as consumers? This question clearly does not have any simple answers. One approach is to take account of their pathways to affluence. In other words, how the affluent and the rich spend their money is in some way influenced by how they got their money in the first place.

Take for instance the inheritance pathway. Most people becoming wealthy through this pathway would very likely have started out in life in relative comfort and material security. Getting an education is unlikely to be a problem. Early familiarity with luxuries would mold the individual's tastes later in life. For them, very often, the big decision is, "Should I join the family business or strike out on my own?"

In contrast, people who become wealthy through the pioneering pathway will have in common a risk-taking attitude, strong self-confidence, a certain amount of aggression (at minimum), and a goal-oriented approach to doing things. They may or may not come from a background of wealth; and they may or may not have a good education. But, having successfully come through the pioneering pathway to affluence, they know that they are successful because of who they are and not because of accidental background circumstances.

The professional pathway to affluence differs from the other two because of its unique prerequisite-education and training. It also differs because it requires a quite highly developed economy and an attendant large and valued service sector. Having strong professional skills is a necessary condition to leverage the professional pathway to affluence. More often than not it also implies that in their working lives their conduct is governed by certain professional standards and rules. They are accustomed to a steady improvement in their material circumstances rather than volatile ups and downs that are the daily fare for risk-taking entrepreneurs.

The influence from the three pathways to affluence certainly does not determine how the affluent and the rich consumers behave. It is just that, an influence. Other factors such as age, gender, lifecycle stages and related personal characteristics remain critically important in understanding consumer behavior. For the affluent and the rich consumers, however, an additional understanding of how they got to be where they are could provide new and useful insights.

Within the context of Asia/Pacific, the region's complex diversity in cultural and social terms will also have to be taken into account. For example, everything else being equal, someone who inherits wealth in Korea may feel compelled to take more seriously the responsibility of doing good for the family than someone in a similar situation in, say, Hong Kong or Sydney. The professional pathway, on the other hand, is likely to function quite differently in China as compared with Japan. In China it is very much a new pathway to affluence, and the young and well educated who are taking advantage of it also tend to be a lot more mobile and "entrepreneurial," and would not hesitate in repeatedly job-hopping. In comparison, Japanese professionals are more accustomed to staying put and working their way up steadily with the same company or in the same professional practice for long periods of time. These market-specific and cultural considerations are important in filling in important details in understanding the affluent and the rich consumers.

Summarizing the above, a number of key concepts useful in capturing the affluent and rich consumers of Asia can be derived. The first concept is "success," the second "convenience," and the third "trust."

Regardless of their specific pathway, the affluent and rich consumers tend to see themselves as successful. Those coming through the pioneering pathway undoubtedly believe that they have been successful, with their experiences of success frequently cast in a heroic mold of risk-taking and David besting Goliath. The affluent and rich professionals may likely see their own success in less flamboyant ways, but more on the basis of one's own solid ability and professionalism. But, it is success all the same. The wealthy consumers endowed with inheritance would also see themselves as successful, regardless of what they actually did or did not do. In their minds, being rich is evidence enough of being successful.

As consumers, these are people who not only want to be treated as being successful, but they would also want to do business with other successful individuals. Thus, a brand will have a strong appeal to them when it is perceived as a flourishing brand. A particular service firm is preferred when the professionals in the firm develop a reputation for achievement. Businesses that are on the up and up will gain their preference. So a useful platform in dealing with the affluent and the rich consumers is "shared success." The company or the brand that does the selling has to come from a position of success, and has to treat the affluent and the rich customers as successes. And, together, they will make each other even more successful.

The watch brand Rolex has clearly positioned itself as such in selling to affluent and rich consumers. In its marketing efforts, Rolex itself as a business is being portrayed as one of long-standing success, while being highly valued by legendary individuals of outstanding successes. Wearing a Rolex watch becomes nothing less than being in a partnership of success.

Secondly, convenience is of supreme importance to the affluent and the rich because time is the one single resource that money cannot buy. Almost by definition the affluent and rich consumers are very busy people. Even the "idle rich" are busy. The idle rich may not have specific work that they have to do each day, but they are typically greatly in demand (and the richer they are the more in demand they become) with social activities and public events of all kinds. The very last thing that they want is to be bothered with what they see as a waste of their time when they go shopping or deal with suppliers of goods and services. Flowery sales pitch is likely to be counter-productive. They want to get to the point right away. They want the supplier to be fully informed, capable of answering all their questions without delay, without asking for help, or checking with superiors. So it is not just a question of catering to the affluent and rich consumers in terms of serving them in the time and place of their convenience (which is important), but being truly knowledgeable, up-to-date in product and service details, and totally prepared for any of their questions.

An industry that has evolved precisely in this direction to capture the affluent and the rich consumers is private banking. This is an industry that has literally taken off in Asia in recent years. Leading players in this industry all exhibit the same characteristics of being able to save their customer's time while addressing their every need and concern professionally, discreetly and satisfactorily.

Finally, there is trust, a core element of business culture across the entire Asia-Pacific region. This is a key concept because of a perennial dilemma faced by the affluent and rich consumers. Most of them pride themselves on being well-informed, and would prefer to make informed decisions whenever possible. But they are also very busy as mentioned above, and hence they do not always have the time to search for the information that they need in order to satisfy themselves that they are making the right decisions on the basis of sufficient knowledge. They therefore need partners that are not only known to be knowledgeable, but also could be trusted. Legal, medical and financial advisors are the traditional careers for serving the affluent and the rich precisely in this capacity. Increasingly, businesses in a variety of personal services are seeking to establish their branding positions in the same way. A successful resort chain, for example, could build its reputation on being trustworthy—consistently delivering quality basics while offering innovative and satisfying experiences that could meet the customer's exacting requirements.

The overriding concept, however, is success. The affluent and the rich consumers are themselves successful. They would also like to be more successful. Businesses that aim to capture these consumers have to become their partners in success. There is nothing that succeeds like success.

ENDNOTES

Chapter 1

1   Bauer, P., 2000, *From Subsistence to Exchange and Other Essays,* New Jersey: Princeton University Press.
2   Baumol, W., *The Free Market Innovation Machine: Analyzing the Growth Miracle of Capitalism.* New Jersey: Princeton University Press.
3   Baumol pointed out that a history of prolific inventions in feudal China had failed to produce commercial innovations precisely because of the lack of private property rights. The state bureaucracy routinely expropriated private invention with no regard to private property rights. Paper was invented by a eunuch, block printing by Buddhist monks, and bill of exchange by businessmen; and all were expropriated by the imperial court without any compensation to the inventors.
4   Hayek, F., 1960, *The Constitution of Liberty,* Chicago: The University of Chicago Press.
5   Loh-Lim, L.L., 2002, *The Blue Mansion: The Story of Mandarin Splendor Reborn,* Penang: L'Plan Sdn Bhd.

Chapter 2

1   The famous fighter plane "zero," which was technically superior to anything that the Allies possessed in the early years of the Pacific War, was designed and manufactured by Mitsubishi.
2   Frederick, J., "The families that own Asia: the Moris," *Time*, February 23, 2004.
3   Hiscock, G. 2000, *Asia's New Wealth Club*, London: Nicholas Brealey Publishing.
4   Frederick, *op. cit.*
5   *Forbes Asia*, June 19, 2006.
6   Hiscock, *op. cit.*
7   See Hedrick-Wong, Y., 2006, *The Glittering Silver Market: the Rise of the Elderly Consumers in Asia*, John Wiley & Sons.
8   Hakuhodo Institute of Life and Living Studies.

Chapter 3

1   Chua, J., *The Sunday Times*, April 30, 2006, Singapore.
2   Roberts, D. and F. Balfour, "To get rich is glorious," *Business Week*. February 6, 2006.
3   *South China Morning Post*, May 29, 2006. P.7.
4   Santini, L., "A new model for success in China," *The Wall Street Journal*. May 12/14, 2006.
5   Sender, H., "China's new class; entrepreneurs," *The Wall Street Journal*. July 17, 2006.
6   Oster, S., *The Wall Street Journal*, May 12/14, 2006.

7 Li, C., 2000, *China's Leaders*: The New Generation. University of Hawaii Press.

8 The survey, a stratified random survey, was conducted between June 2005 and May 2006, covering 15,000 respondents with annual income exceeding $10,000. The survey was jointly designed by MasterCard Asia/Pacific and the China National Research Association (CNRA), and carried out by survey teams from CNRA. CNRA was established in 1991 by the national Bureau of Statistics of China, the Development Research Center of the State Council, and the Chinese Academy of Social Sciences. It is managed by the national Bureau of Statistics. The 10 cities surveyed are Beijing, Shanghai, Guangzhou, Tianjin, Chengdu, Chongqing, Wuhan, Nanjing, Shenzhen, and Hangzhou.

Chapter 4

1 Das, G., 2000, *India Unbound*, Penguin Books.

2 *Ibid*

3 Cited in Yergin, D. and J. Stanislaw, 1998, *The Commanding Heights*, New York: Simon & Schuster.

4 Lala, R,M., 1992, *Beyond the Last Blue Mountain - A Life of J.R.D. Tata*, Penguin Books.

5 Hiscock, G., 2000, *Asia's New Wealth Club*, London: Nicholas Brealey.

6 These elite institutions come with a price, the unfortunate neglect of basic education for the majority Indians, especially those in rural areas, a situation demanding urgent reform today.

7 Moreau, R. and Mazumdar S., "Bigger, Faster, and Better," *Newsweek*, July 17, 2006.

8 Other leading names of Marwari businesses include Bajbaj (auto), Ruta (steel and oil), Jindal (power and oil), Agarwal (mining). The Birlas are also of Marwari descent.

9 Glader, P. and Bellman E., "Mittal trades control for growth," *Asian Wall Street Journal*, July 10, 2006.

10 Asher, M.G., "Whither the Indian Diaspora in the 21st century," *Business Times* (Singapore), July 1998.

11 In 2004 US dollars.

12 McKinsey India estimates.

Chapter 5

1 Australian Bureau of Statistics.

2 Australian Bureau of Statistics, *Small Businesses in Australia, 2005*.

3 *Forbes Asia* estimate.

4 *Ibid*

Chapter 6

1 The fourth is Singapore, addressed in the next chapter.

2 Stern, J., Kim J.H., Perkins D.H., and Yoo J.H., 1995, *Industrialization and the State: The Korean Heavy and Chemical Industry Drive*. Cambridge, Mass.: Harvard Institute for International Development.

3 Schuman, M., "The Miracle Workers," *Time*, August 6, 2005.

4 Wade, R., 1990, *Governing the Market: Economic Theory and the Role of Government in East Asian Industrialization*, Princeton: Princeton University Press.

5 Li, K.T., 1995, *The Evolution behind Taiwan's Development Success*, Singapore: World Scientific Publishing.

6 Hedrick-Wong, Y., Kumar, Y.S., Siddique S., 2005, *Mind the Gap: Singapore Investment in China*, Singapore: Institute of Southeast Asian Studies.

7 Friedman, M., 1990, *Free to Choose*, Chicago: University of Chicago Press.

8 Vogel, E.F., 1991, *The Four Little Dragons: The Spread of Industrialization in East Asia*, Cambridge Mass.: Harvard University Press.

9 Net worth estimated at $18.8 billion, according to *Forbes Asia* in 2005.

10 Gill, A., 2006, *The Next Generation*, CLSA.

11 Smith, P.L., "Family-run firms greet MBA era in Hong Kong", *International Herald Tribune*, July 18, 2006.

Chapter 7

1 ASEAN stands for the "Association of Southeast Asian Nations," and consists of 10 members today.

2 For details, see Church, P. (ed.), 2006, *A Short History of Southeast Asia*, (4th edition) Singapore: John Wiley & Sons.

3 Seagrave, S., 1995, *Lords of the Rim*, London: Bantam Press.

4 Huff, W.G., 1997, *The Economic Growth of Singapore: Trade & Development in the 20th Century*, Cambridge: Cambridge University Press.

5 Hiscock, G., 2000, *Asia's New Wealth Club*, London: Nicholas Brealey Publishers.

6 The World Bank, 2000, *Malaysia: Social and Structural Review Update*, Washington, D.C.

7 It was overtaken by Shanghai's Pudong Telecom Tower, which was in turn overtaken by the 101 Building in Taipei, Taiwan, which is today's tallest building in the world.

8 Church, P., (ed.) 2006, *A Short History of Southeast Asia*, Singapore: John Wiley & Sons (Asia).

9 Hiscock, *op. cit.*

10 Church, *op. cit.*

11 Data from *Forbes Asia*, 2005.

12 World Bank data.

13 Hutchcroft, P. D., 1998, *Booty Capitalism: the Politics of Banking in the Philippines*, Manila: Ateneo De Manila University Press.

14 De Soto, H., 2000, *The Mystery of Capital*, New York: Basic Books.

Chapter 8

1 These trend rates of real GDP growth are also summarized in the appendix.

INDEX

OTHER MASTERCARD TITLES

0-470-82206-6
February 2006

Holding up Half of the Sky:
The New Women Consumers of Asia
Describes the dynamics of the rising
power of women consumers in 11
countries in Asia. It looks at how
women's changing roles in society are
fundamentally altering their roles as
consumers.

0-470-82207-4
September 2006

The Glittering Silver Market: The Rise of
the Elderly Consumers in Asia examines
the current elderly consumer markets
in Japan, Korea, China, Taiwan, Hong
Kong SAR, India, Singapore, Malaysia,
Thailand, Indonesia, the Philippines and
Australia; and forecasts where they will
be in 10 years' time.